PRAISE FOR ONE WITH GOD

"A subject as wondrous as our Creator God and as breathtaking as the fact that we can experience true oneness with him deserves a treatment this inspiring, this biblically grounded, and this beautifully written."

— **Tim Challies**, Christian pastor, blogger, and author of several books, including *Visual Theology*, *Epic*, and *Seasons of Sorrow*

"One reason the modern emphasis on the self is so sinister is God made us for union with him. Union with the living God in Christ — almost too good to be true! — is a powerful tonic against the subtle, destructive spells of our age. Drink deeply of this book. That is, slowly, without hurry, and, as much as you're able, without distraction. And do what God made us, as humans, uniquely for: meditate on God and marvel."

– **David Mathis**, senior teacher, desiringGod.org; pastor, Cities Church, Saint Paul, Minnesota; author, *Workers for Your Joy: The Call of Christ on Christian Leaders*

"*One with God* is a personal, poetic, practical and potent primer for spiritual growth. Herein Pierce Hibbs imparts theological nourishment to refocus, refresh and restore souls by deepening our understanding and experience of union with Christ."
– **Dr. Peter A. Lillback**, president, Westminster Theological Seminary, Philadelphia

"This book is a wonder-filled, thoughtful combination of rich theology, poetic expression, personal sensitivity, and spiritual devotion. It unfolds how to pursue God in the light of his pursuit of us. Read it and taste the love of God."
– **Vern S. Poythress**, Distinguished Professor of New Testament, Biblical Interpretation, and Systematic Theology, Westminster Theological Seminary

"One with God presents the reader with 12 concise chapters of mediations by Pierce Hibbs on Jesus's great prayer of John 17. Each chapter takes up a theme of being One with God that Hibbs then develops. Most profitable is that every chapter concludes with reflection questions, prayer, and reader resources that allow the reader to apply what he has learned. A very beautiful series of mediations on Jesus's High Priestly prayer, suitable for individual or group discussions."

— **Rev. Dr. Alfred Poirier**, Professor of Pastoral Theology, Westminster Theological Seminary, PA

"In some ways, this book's thesis is simple: *Chase after God*. What could be sweeter or more relevant at a time when we seem to be chasing anything and everything else. This is the message that can change our life and Pierce Hibbs has articulated it so thoughtfully here."

— **Michael Horton**, J. Gresham Machen Professor, Westminster Seminary California

"Gracious words are like a honeycomb, sweetness to the soul and health to the body." So writes the sage in Proverbs 16:24. In *One with God*, Pierce Hibbs provides such wise and winning words for your faith. Like a chef de cuisine, Hibbs takes the life-giving doctrines of the Holy Trinity and union with Christ, adds pinches of life's seasoning and fresh illustrations, to produce a scrumptious, nutritious meal. No more will the Triune God and union with Jesus remain on an upper shelf as surely-important but out-of-reach sustenance. In *One with God*, you will join Hibbs in feast and fellowship around a table of grace, complete with rich, relevant, and rewarding truth. Pull up a chair and join in this delightfully accessible meal; enter into sweet and dynamic communion with the One who is himself our life."

— **David B. Garner**, Vice President of Global Ministries and Professor of Systematic Theology, Westminster Theological Seminary

"There could be no more important virtue than being one. Pierce Hibbs helpfully argues that the essence of biblical oneness is love. He names and resolves the many obstacles to unity, be they psychological or philosophical. Readers will be pleasantly surprised to discover there are fresh ways to describe a tried and true gift from God. Rich and deeply satisfying, *One with God* should be read, slowly and carefully. In that great blessings await."

– **William Edgar**, Professor of Apologetics, Westminster Theological Seminary

ONE WITH GOD

Finding Your Identity, Purpose, and Destiny in the God Who Speaks

Pierce Taylor Hibbs

Truth Ablaze

Copyright © 2023 by Pierce Taylor Hibbs

All rights reserved.

No portion of this book may be reproduced in any form without written permission from the publisher or author, except as permitted by U.S. copyright law.

Hardcover ISBN: 979-8-9861067-6-2

Paperback ISBN: 979-8-9861067-7-9

Scripture quotations are from the ESV® Bible (The Holy Bible, English Standard Version®), copyright © 2001 by Crossway, a publishing ministry of Good News Publishers. Used by permission. All rights reserved.

CONTENTS

Dedication	IX
Foreword	X
1. Yearning for Oneness	1
2. What Is Oneness?	14
3. Begin Where You Are	21
4. The God of Oneness	39
5. The Prayer of Prayers	59
6. You Were Made for This	75
7. The Absence of Oneness	85
8. The Path to Oneness	107
9. Oneness in Private	136
10. Oneness in Public	163
11. The Day Eternal	173
Epilogue	177
Also by the author	182

Endnotes

For Bonz Hart, whose faithfulness to the Lord in the midst of cancer has only given me a greater yearning for my eternal oneness with God. Thank you, my friend, for lifting high the torch of hope.

FOREWORD

One with God is a short book, but it is no "quick read"—because the author, who is a careful theologian and wordsmith, has taken the time to approach a complex and pulsing subject and make it memorably clear for the head and the heart. Slice the book's pages almost anywhere and the reader will find lines like "to soar on the thermals of grace" and "Our oneness with God is the beating heart of our existence, thudding to a rhythm that has no end." So, be prepared for an engaging read! Pierce has also given careful attention to crafting the structure of the book's eleven chapters, so as to enhance the impact on his readers. Each chapter ends with reflection questions, a crafted prayer, and some with the author's poems or further Reader Resources.

The thrust of the book (in a *reductionist* nutshell) is the dizzying reality that we Christians have been granted *oneness* with God, and that Christ has petitioned the Father that our *oneness* be brought to full fruition (John 17: 11, 21-23)—and that this *oneness* (when lived out) will draw the world to Christ (17:23) and, further, that our *oneness* will deepen our joyous certitude of Christ's words as to our ultimate destiny.

As an exacting trinitarian theologian, the author has written elsewhere on the Trinity,[1] and here he focuses his understanding on the subject of oneness. The Trinity is profoundly one because each person of the Godhead lives in the others. Of this Pierce beautifully writes: "The oneness of the Father, Son, and Spirit in love, power, and joy burns brighter than a thousand suns... in eternity. There is no such thing as a time when this was not. This is infinite oneness with unparalleled intimacy." From all eternity there has always been continual exchange, sharing, ultimate fellowship, and oneness.

This is the dazzling background for Jesus's petition to the Father, "that that they may all be one, just as you, Father are in me, and I in you, that they also may be in us, so that the world may believe that you have sent me" (John 17:23). It is an intra-trinitarian prayer. God prays to God—that's all! Trinitarian certitude. This means that our oneness, and our heart's desire for oneness, is divinely ordained and implanted. All God's children are endowed with an ineluctable longing for oneness.

Midway through the book, the author gives practical reasons for the absence of oneness in the lives of believers, focusing on the theological causes: *disobedience*, *fear* and *shame*, along with their biblical antidotes. He then lists practical down-to-earth causes beginning with *hurry* as a "corrosive disease," listing ten penetrating symptoms of "hurry sickness." Next is *distraction*, identifying the smartphone as the ubiquitous culprit: "the average American checks his phone once every ten minutes. That's 96 times a day." He then deals with *lesser loves,* lesser lights that detract us from the Father of light. And then, of course, *lies* regarding the reality and presence of God, a problem as old as the Garden.

The book then moves from diagnosis to a prescription for oneness, providing a road map to monitor our own steps on the path, beginning with a map for the private life ("Oneness in Private: Cultivating Communion") and then a map for the public life. The result of cultivating both private oneness and public oneness is evangelism: "so that the world may believe that you have sent me" (John 17:21). The gospel will go forth in both its drawing-saving power and repelling-condemning power. Our lives will radiate gospel power.

Reading and re-reading *One with God* was good for my head and my heart. The fact that as Christians we have been granted to share in the eternal oneness of the Holy Trinity, a oneness without beginning and without end, and of unparalleled intimacy, is hard to get into my head. But, what I do understand is mind-blowing, and the more I understand the more my heart is filled with awe and love. And this, coupled with Jesus's prayer (God praying to God for our oneness) has enhanced my soul's certitude and longing for oneness and, of course, the will to chase after it.

Indeed, this little book is no quick read, but rather a book to slowly and prayerfully read again and again.

– **R. Kent Hughes**

CHAPTER ONE

YEARNING FOR ONENESS

The sun is rising. The pale and glorious gold is turning whiter behind the swaying arms of the maple trees. The robins—they keep singing, as if their songs were lifting light up from the horizon, pushing it through the tiny windows of the canopy, pouring gold over the green. Above the trees, the clouds are scudding silent and serene, like children content not to speak. They're going somewhere. My heart wishes it could travel with them, fall into the flock of mist and morning mirth, drift above the rambling Pennsylvania countryside. Two blue jays yell over the yard, and a truck engine churns through the quiet. The world is awake. The rhythm of Monday is stepping into the foreground. Soon I'll be moving. Soon I'll be speaking. Soon I'll be lifting and pulling and typing. But before the day gets on, I sit here with my pen, waiting for a thermal.

I've always envied birds. I think it's because I have a deep-seated belief that souls were meant to soar. I love watching the robins and the wrens dart across the treetops, flapping with their hollow-boned freedom from pine bough to maple limb. But it's the red-tailed hawks that capture me most. I see them open-armed and circling as they rise up. They don't even need to flap because thermals lift them. They rise on invisible shoulders. They rise on unseen grace. They rise on gifts.

As I sit at the table with dawn peering over my shoulders, I realize that's what I'm waiting for—a thermal. I'm waiting for the unseen Spirit to give me some words. And in that giving, I know I will rise to new heights. I'll be raised. All I need to do is keep my arms out.

Mystical, isn't it? I used to think these dreams were the result of a boy's mind being trapped in a man's body (maybe that's still true). But now I believe it's more than that. It's about longing. It's about living. It's about . . . destiny. I dream of flying with the birds because my heart has tasted the wildness of God. I want *him*, and he is high. Above the sky. Above the scudding clouds—light beyond light. On this earth, my neck will always be craning upwards. I'll always stare at the birds because I'm in love with the one who cares for them. I want to get higher, closer. I want to go, as C. S. Lewis said, "further up and further in."[2] I want to go so high and so deep that I'm one with the God of red-tails. *One.* That's what this book is about.

Made for Oneness

We were made for oneness with God. It's who we are, not just what we want. Everything in us, as Geerhardus Vos put it, is "disposed for communion."[3] Communion is relational oneness with God. There's no running from this, no more than a house could run from its foundation. It's in the marrow of our bones. It's silently dwelling among every synapse of thought. It's in our eyes as we gaze at the teeming world around us. It's in every knuckle bend and muscle movement. Everything that is you is somehow longing for, reaching for, hoping for oneness with God.

Our world raves about identity, about the unbound freedom to create and define ourselves. But they have missed this. Our identity is not primarily about us—what we do, what we think, what we like. It's primarily about the God who made us for himself. Sounds strange, I know. But that's because most people are what John Calvin might have called letters Cs. They're curved in on themselves. And when you're curved in on yourself, you can't see the horizon your soul is sailing towards. There is something beyond us that defines us. And I believe that thing is oneness with God.

Destined for Oneness

But being one with God isn't only about identity. It's also about *destiny*, about where we're going. That's a hard concept to grasp in the ordinary moments of the day, isn't it? When you're folding dish towels. When you're writing an email. When you're paying bills. String enough of those routine moments together, and a concept like *destiny* turns into a vapor, evaporating in the burning light of the immediate. Destiny seems at home in epic fantasy, but a strange ghost in our daily lives.

That doesn't mean it's not there. We need to think of destiny as the sun behind our clouds. Just because we don't see it doesn't mean it's not there, that it's not pulling all things toward itself, that it's not illuminating every blade of grass and every dust fiber of our ordinary moments. Our destiny is like the sun. We're mostly unaware of it, and yet it engulfs and surrounds all that we do, all that we are.

What, more plainly, is our destiny? It's oneness with God, but what does that even mean? We'll unpack that in this book, but for now, think of it this way: *Our destiny is to speak with God and see his face without interruption.* Speech and sight, communion and presence, sharing and staring at the one who *is* love, the one who knows you better than your mother or father, better than you know yourself. Our destiny is to speak and see our heavenly Father, his eternal Son, and the life-giving Holy Ghost. *Here*, we search for the three in great frustration. *There*, we'll be with them as our destination. It's a destination with a beginning but no end, a conversation that starts but never stops, a love-gaze with an inception but no conclusion. It's, as Lewis had it, "Chapter One of the Great Story which no one on earth has read."[4] What could a human imagination do to honor such a Great Story but build a block tower or cover a piece of paper with crayon scribbles? Before this destiny, we're all children. We're all tiny. We don't even know how to dream of it.

But do we know how to *yearn* for it anymore? And if not, what are we doing here? How can we walk through the world without gripping our destiny with both hands?

The short answer: we create counterfeits.[5] And we're *very* good at it. The greatest counterfeiters are masters of deception. They take what *isn't* and offer it as what *is*. And we believe them, even if the counterfeiter is our own soul. John Calvin wasn't being hyperbolic when he said our hearts are idol factories.[6] He might also have said that we're master counterfeiters.

A counterfeit, spiritually speaking, is anything that absorbs our attention other than God and his work. I say "absorbs" because a counterfeit isn't designed to be "mostly substitutionary." It's designed to take the place of the original. Like a dry sponge, it soaks up all of our attention and energy. There's no remainder. We're left without yearning, without a passion for oneness with God.

Anything can be a counterfeit because anything can be an idol, and counterfeits are the latest in idol technology. With ancient idols, it was obvious people were worshiping something other than the invisible God, that they were giving their lives to something else. But the power of the counterfeit comes in its suggestion of being harmless, of being "just a thing." Coffee. Exercise. Ambition. Sex. Clothes. These aren't idols; they're just things, right? . . . Right?

If any one of these little things gives you more energy and passion and joy than being one with God does, you have an idol, a counterfeit. And we take idol currency without even checking for authenticity. "It's just coffee!" we say with an eye-roll. But we spend a great deal of time with our pour-over technique, our coffee bean subscriptions, our routine grinding and brewing. More time, perhaps, than we give to think about the God who grew the coffee plants, who shaped the harvesters after his own image, whose common grace lends us the machinery for roasting and the planes for shipping.

In vs. Elsewhere

"So, I can't be a coffee connoisseur?!" No. That's not what I'm saying. I'm saying that there's a difference between *in* and *elsewhere*. You can find God *in* coffee; you can see him *in* the details—his nature and grace. That is, you can see God's nature reflected in all the things that he's made (Rom. 1:20).[7] Or you can decide, even tacitly, that he can only be seen *elsewhere*. If you decide that God can only be seen elsewhere, then you see your coffee passion as "just a coffee thing." You see it as detached from or even void of God-reflection. And that's where the power of the counterfeit lives.

See, our counterfeits aren't claiming to be gods, as the ancient idols did. No—they're claiming instead to be "just things." But they take from us the exact same resources that ancient idols did: our time, energy, passion, and praise. Do you see it? Do you see how the latest in idol technology pulls us so effectively away from our yearning for oneness with God?

We take these counterfeits—almost every day—and block our own view of God-given destiny. We say flippantly, deep down in our hearts, "This is why I'm here." Or, if you think that's too strong, we keep saying, "I'll find God *elsewhere*, not right now. Not in this. I'll just enjoy this for what it is."[8]

And then two problems take root. First, we never find a place for "elsewhere." God becomes practically irrelevant to us. We say he's our destiny, but we don't live like it. Second, we believe the lie that *anything* could be what it is apart from God. God has created the world so that everything reflects something of his divine nature (Rom. 1:20; Ps. 19:1–4). Everything. There's no such thing as "just coffee." God is revealing himself in every stage of the plant growth, the harvesting, the drying, the roasting, the brewing. God upholds every coffee bean by the word of his power (Heb. 1:3). There's no such thing as "just coffee." Do you see the counterfeit now?

We're daily counterfeiters. We live for a thousand tiny gods. Throughout the day, we functionally express the little claim, "This is why I'm here." But "this" never seems to be oneness with God.

We're going to reclaim our identity, purpose, and destiny in this book. We're going to assault the practice of counterfeiting. Watch your back, Satan.

The Path to Oneness

But how? Oneness with God doesn't just tell us who we are and where we're going. It also tells us how we'll get there. And so now we have the three points from the subtitle of the book: *identity*, *purpose*, and *destiny*. If you want question words, it would be *who*, *why*, and *where*.

Whenever you're traveling somewhere, you need a place to stay. You need a home away from home. You need somewhere to dwell, an abode to abide in. And we have that home not in a place but in a *person*. Jesus said, "Abide in me, and I in you. As the branch cannot bear fruit by itself unless it abides in the vine, neither can you, unless you abide in me" (John 15:4). Jesus calls us to *live* in him. That's deeply mysterious, isn't it? He's not saying, "Think highly of me" or "worship me," though we're called to do that, too. He's saying, "*live* in me." If our destiny is oneness with God, Jesus is saying, "Live in me until you get there." What could this possibly mean? How do we explain this mystery?

I find myself agreeing with Rankin Wilbourne. "Explaining a mystery is like explaining a joke. If you do that, you kill it."[9] But he also says, "You are more and most yourself when united to Christ. He covers you, he shields you, he represents you before the Father. He also fills you, illuminates you, and animates you, making you more yourself and more human than you could ever be on your own."[10] There's still mystery here. Trying to get away from the mystery of living *in* another person is sort of like trying to get away from the air while you breathe it. You can almost imagine what that's like, but even while you try, the air is around you and inside you. Maybe a poem would help.

Christ, you told me that I live in you.

You said you are the vine.
I'm still me, and you're still you.
I'm still human; you're divine.
But you are now a home to me.
I live inside your walls.
You shelter as you set me free
To answer holy calls.

Well, maybe that doesn't help so much, if by "help" we mean "explain." *Help* in a deeper sense, however, doesn't mean rationalization. *Help* doesn't mean we wrap our minds around it. *Help* means we worship. We glory in the truth. We smile in the secret.

We'll explore this mystery later in the book. For now, my point is that oneness with God—living *in* Christ by the power of the Holy Spirit—is how we get to oneness with God. See the circularity? The gospel is full of that. Want an example? The *Word* took on flesh to save us, who rejected God's *words*, so that we might live in God's *Word* again and be joined with the God who spoke us. Circularity. It's not ridiculous; it's mysterious. And there's a difference. Something ridiculous gets us nowhere and leaves us with nothing. Something mysterious gets us somewhere and leaves us with everything. Think of it as a couplet:

Ridiculous makes no sense and lets us roam.
Mysterious opens a fence and points us home.

Somehow the mystery of being one with God is our identity, our destiny, and our path. That's what this book is about.

I start with an invitation, a call. Why should you read this book? Why might you even (dare I say?) *re*-read it? If you long for a deeper relationship with the God who speaks, this book is for you. If you're tired of living as if your faith is just a set of ideas that you agree with, this book is for you. If you want to have confidence and security in your identity, if you want to reclaim your sense of purpose, if you yearn for something to help you live closer to God on a daily basis, then this book is for you. I'll be candid with you. *I* want all these things, so this book is for *me* too. Let's start this conversation in pages with a prayer.

> God, we want you.
> Really. Just you.
> We want you to illuminate
> And define us.
> We want you to give us
> Passion and purpose for you.
> We want to be one with you,
> Just as Jesus prayed for.
> Give us the eyes to see it,
> The ears to hear it,
> And the heart to grasp it.
> May we never let it go,
> As you never let us go.

Now, we can start our conversation together by delving more deeply into what oneness with God really is. Then we'll be in a good place to talk about who we are, who God is, and where we're going as "the world spins madly on" (The Weepies).

Reflection Questions and Prayer

1. What are some things that you *yearn* for today? Make a short list. Why do you yearn for them? What value do they offer you?

2. Think of a "counterfeit" in your own life. What does that counterfeit offer you but not ultimately give you?

3. How do you think oneness with God grows in your daily life?

4. What do you think of when you hear the word "destiny"? How do you think most people respond to that word? Why do you think they respond that way?

5. Write down one thing you hope to get from this book, a change you hope to see. Return to this when you reach the end.

Prayer
God, we're out of practice in simply yearning for you.

Out identity blurs at the edges.
Our purpose evaporates among a million details.
Our destiny is a light eclipsed by clouds.
We need you.
We want to be *one* with you.
We want closeness to be our calling.
Help us to focus our hearts
So that we magnify you,
So that your beauty grows like a garden,
Surrounding our ordinary moments.
Keep us in the garden of your greatness.

Reader Resource: The Original and the Counterfeits

I mentioned in this chapter the idea of *counterfeits*. Our lives are filled with counterfeits, and we're mostly unaware of them. That's because counterfeits are designed to go undetected; they're made to be invisible. Satan, the master counterfeiter and father of lies (John 8:44), doesn't want us to see what he's up to, how he's tricking our hearts to fall into relationships that promise and never deliver. You might use the table below to identify the counterfeits in your own life. Note in the first row what God says we should focus on. I've offered an example of a counterfeit and then given you space to track some of your own.

The Original or Counterfeit	What It Offers	What It Does	Where It Leads Us
THE TRIUNE GOD	Eternal love and value, peace beyond understanding, and an identity rooted in holiness	Makes us more like Christ, the image of the invisible God	To God himself, who is our ultimate destiny
MATERIAL POSSESSIONS	Temporary enjoyment and a sense of satisfaction, a vapor of peace, a disappearing identity	Trains us to seek out more things, to embrace a never-ending cycle of seeking and getting, helping us to ignore our mortality	To exhaustion and frustration as we realize the cycle never ends

Chapter Two

WHAT IS ONENESS?

Later in the book, we'll be unpacking oneness in the context of Jesus's high priestly prayer (John 17). In fact, that passage will be the jewel we stare at for many of these pages. But we need somewhere to start, a general idea of what God means when he calls us to be one with him.

It may not jump out to you right away, since oneness sounds abstract, but oneness is really all about love. Oneness is an expression of intimacy, a circle that encloses persons in deep relationship. This is what we want more than anything: to be fully known and loved for eternity.

Most people spend their entire lives searching for that in other people. They're looking for the oneness of love, even though they wouldn't call it that. But this oneness of love is high, so high that we can't get to it all on our own. It's the peak of Everest that we can't ascend by ourselves. The fully satisfying oneness of love comes from above us, since God is the origin. God, after all, is love (1 John 4:8). God is perfect, intimate, personal relationship. Our longing for the oneness of love will never be satisfied apart from him.

The Romanian Orthodox theologian Dumitru Stănlioae once wrote,

> God does not need our love in the same way that we need His. And this is a result of the limited nature of humans. This is why we are helped to grow in love's infinity and in the joy that comes from loving our fellow men more and more, in the joy that comes from loving others more and more. Still, however many people we love, none of them can truly satisfy us, and none can assure us eternal beatitude, for they cannot open us up to an infinite love. Like us, they remain thirsty for a loving relationship with the Triune God.[11]

I love the wording "opens us up." Sometimes human souls resemble clams more than their Creator. They're shut tight, clamped and closed, not wanting the light. And only divine hands can pry them open to reveal what's inside. And what's inside is longing for what's outside. The God without beginning or end is the God of love, and it's him that we want most. He is the oneness of love that invites us into eternal relationship. And it starts now.

Oneness: Truth, Trust, and Speech

So, oneness is shorthand for love and relationship, for fellowship. And oneness requires truth, trust, and speech.

Let's start with truth. You can't be one with someone you don't truly know. The truth—about who you are, what you're like, what your passions are—has to be set on the table before the one you love. Everything is open. Everything is exposed. Truth is the door to oneness.

Trust comes once we reach out to open the door. Trust is laying our life down in the shadow of another. It's saying, "I am willing to place my hopes, my welfare, and my identity in your hands. I may not be able to see everything, but I see you, and that's enough." Trust is the path of oneness.

Speech—what I call communion behavior—is what holds oneness together.[12] Oneness is a fellowship of persons, and fellowship is born in the country of communion—that place where sharing and expression are the air we breathe. Speech is the atmosphere of oneness.

We've all had trouble with truth, trust, and speech throughout our lives, haven't we? And that means we've had trouble with oneness, with love and divine relationship. Something is broken. But what's been broken has also been repaired by the God of oneness.

Start with truth again. In Eden, our ancestors rejected the truth about God—his goodness and prodigal heart. To remedy that, God would eventually send himself, as the truth (John 14:16), to earth's doorstep. The truth of who God is—the person of truth—would set the door of oneness before us again. In Jesus Christ, we find the oneness of love. As Timothy Jennings wrote, "Life, health and happiness are only found where love flows free. And love only flows free where the truth about God is known!"[13] God didn't just reveal the truth with pen and paper. He didn't just send a message. The message was the messenger. The truth is a person. We enter oneness with God through him. It's beautifully simple for Jesus to tell us he is "the door" (John 10:9). He's the most wonderful door the world has ever seen.

Trust, which was broken by us, was also restored through Christ. All throughout John's Gospel we're called to trust that God sent his Son. And trust trickles down to us from a divine spring. The Sender (the Father) calls for our trust by bringing his Son (the Sent) to us in the white-doved, winged presence of the Holy Spirit (John 1:32). We trust the sender by trusting the one he sent in the power of his sending.

But this trust is a work of God for us, in us. He doesn't leave us to ourselves. He meets us where we are and carries us where we need to go, all so that we might be with him where he is (John 14:3). Trust, like everything else, is a gift. Just as truth is. Just as the speech of God is. God is always giving.[14]

Along with truth and trust, the oneness of love is completed by speech. There can be no oneness without sharing, without expression. And God spoke (and speaks) creatively and redemptively.

We know God created all things through speech, but we overlook the redemption that follows Adam and Eve's rebellion. It comes in a little question in Genesis: "Where are you?" (Gen. 3:9) Silence is judgment. Speech is grace. God could've stopped his lips and left us alone in the garden forever. But he didn't. He spoke. That's grace.

And stare more closely at this question in Genesis 3:9. God is all-knowing. He doesn't need to ask where they are. So, why does he do it? He's addressing the oneness broken by rebellion, by a lack of trust and a following of falsehood, a chasing after counterfeits. He's starting the conversation again. He's setting before them the door to oneness: the Word. Most theologians point out the first glimmer of the gospel in Genesis 3:15. But it comes before that. It comes in this little question: Where are you?

Again, given what we know about God, he couldn't have been asking the question to obtain information. He wasn't asking to learn; he was asking to love. He was inviting them back into oneness. Can you see it?

Pause here for a moment of application. In Christ, God asks this question of us continually, in the silent syllables of his Spirit. "Where are you?" Right now. Go on. Answer it. It's not a trick. Where are you right now, spiritually? Where are you? God already knows. He's just waiting for you to come out of your ridiculous hiding place and say, "I'm over here." So often in our spiritual lives we act as if God doesn't truly know where we are going or where we are. He already knows. He's not looking for you because he's never lost sight of you in the first place. Wherever you are right now, voice it to God. That's the beginning of oneness.

We'll touch on these themes again throughout the book. For now, I just wanted to give us a starting point for understanding what oneness is. Oneness is a relationship of love fostered through truth, trust, and speech.

But this is only the beginning of the book. The problem we'll be working through together is why this oneness is fleeting for us, and how we can receive divine help in restoring it and keeping it central in our daily lives.

To do all that, we need to begin where we are. Right now. In this moment. Where are you? We'll pick up the next chapter with that question.

Reflection Questions and Prayer

1. Oneness with God means that we're made to be in relationship with him. How does that truth contrast with various counterfeit gods of our culture?

2. Think of truth, trust, and speech in some of your human relationships. What problems do you see? Are some of these problems mirrored in your relationship with God?

3. Identify an obstacle to trusting in God. It could be "not knowing the future" or "trusting what you can see more than what you can't." How does that obstacle keep you from a full and open relationship with God?

Prayer

God of relationship,

We are yours.

We're made for your truth,

To trust in your words,

To live in your environment (Acts 17:28).

But we have trouble following the truth,

Trusting your voice,

Holding on to your words

In a noisy world.

Help us to stop for a moment.

Help us to stare at the truth:

You know and love us fully;

You gave yourself for us;

You're preparing a place for us;

You want all of us . . . today.

Give us the courage

To challenge what competes

For the pinnacle of our hope, love, and fulfillment.

Chapter Three
BEGIN WHERE YOU ARE

Spiritual concepts can make me feel small and remote. When the words "oneness with God" enter my ears, I can only think about how far from this I feel. "One with God? Do I ever feel that way?" That—right there—is a trick of our culture, a trick of human thought. We're raised in an environment that tells us *feeling = truth*. If you can't *feel* something, then it must not *be* something. At best, if you can't feel something, then it must only be an idea, not a reality. We make feelings final. Experience is a close second. But the promises of God? They become tertiary, if we're lucky.

Make no mistake, if we think this way, we're going to be lost. Perhaps you even feel a little lost right now. We all do at times. Let me help you be found.

For much of this book, we'll be drawing water from the well of John 17, Jesus's high priestly prayer. But look at some verses in John 14 for a moment.

> "If you love me, you will keep my commandments. And I will ask the Father, and he will give you another Helper, to be with you forever, even the Spirit of truth, whom the world cannot receive, because it neither sees him nor knows him. You know him, for he dwells with you and will be in you." (John 14:15–17)

> "If anyone loves me, he will keep my word, and my Father will love him, and we will come to him and make our home with him." (John 14:23)

We talked briefly about oneness as a loving relationship. And here we have Jesus telling us that a loving relationship lives in us. Because we love Jesus, the Father gives us the Holy Spirit, who makes us his home. Think about that. The moment you believed in Jesus Christ, the Spirit fluttered down and said, "Ah, a new home. Let me get settled in this one."

But that home—your soul—isn't vacant when the Spirit moves in. Apparently, the Father and the Son are long-term residents. A party of three is eternally living in you. Right now. Regardless of what you *feel*, your heart is the home of the Trinity! Even as I write these words, they are beyond me. Can they really be true? Could the all-powerful God live inside such a fragile house? Can the sun live within a grain of dust?

Well, the God who *is* truth, the God who cannot lie (Titus 1:2), said it. So, it *must* be true. Whether or not you and I *feel* this is secondary. Truth is the foundation upon which feelings play, like swallows in barn rafters, swooping and darting from beam to beam. Feelings are fun; we love watching the swallows in the rafters. They have an excited energy. But they play *upon* something else. There's no such thing as pure feeling. Feeling always sets its hollow-boned body on the edges of wood, and that wood is either rotting (lies) or living (truth), taken from the massive root bulb of the vine-dressing God. Feelings are not and never will be a foundation. They flutter.

I'm saying all this up front because we're so prone to thinking of feelings as foundational. They're not. Feelings always dance upon something else. They're barn swallows, not the barn's framework.

So, what do we do? Let's start by recognizing that barn swallows dip and dive. They go up and down, just as our feelings, just as our experiences. We have an inherent hatred of this reality. We don't want to rise and fall. We want to rise and stay. We want oneness with God to *feel* true and invigorating all the time.

Mountain Climbers on a Heart Monitor

Another way of thinking about this is to use two images: a heart monitor and the embedded image of each one of us climbing up the peaks and valleys of that monitor like a mountaineer. Let's start with the heart monitor.

Put your hand on your chest. Keep it there for a few moments.

That soft pulsing—do you know what that is? It's the body's electricity.[15] Like the rest of your muscles, your heart can conduct electrical pulses. It actually has a natural pacemaker that sends out electrical waves. Those waves make the heart muscles contract, first those in the upper chamber, then those in the lower (about a quarter of a second later). This happens about 50–100 times a minute, depending on who you are and what you're doing.

No one thinks about this. Instead, we just function. Each week, our bodies waltz through a sequence of seconds like leaves blown through blades of grass on a fallow field. We're only aware of our heart beat when we're scared or excited or covered in sweat, when this four-chambered drum in our chest is thudding out our existence, pumping oxygen through tiny rivers beneath our skin. In other words, we notice our heart only in peaks and valleys—good and bad. When we exert ourselves, we notice ourselves.

Something similar happens in our spiritual lives, only we'd have to replace our heart beat with the life-giving Spirit of God, the song that's been quietly sung ever since we gasped for air and entered a world of light and sound. God's Spirit has put breath in our lungs and vigor in our veins (Gen. 2:7; Job 33:4), but we only notice him when trouble remains, when suffering lingers, when hope dries up.[16] Or, conversely, we notice him when we're full of passion and mirth, when voices are singing silent night in a room with a hundred candles, when the eulogy we hear calls up phantoms of ambition and regret, when our five-year-old hugs us without our asking, just because. That's when we notice the Spirit within our spirit. That's when we feel our soul's heart beating, drumming to a pace set in eternity past, directing our gaze to eternity future. As the writer of Ecclesiastes put it, God buried eternity in our hearts (Eccl. 3:11). Sometimes it's buried deeper than we wish.

The downside to all this is simple: When we're not exerting ourselves spiritually, we have a hard time noticing God, and the truth of our oneness with him fades into the background. Without peaks and valleys in the soul's heart monitor, we flatline. We stop breathing. We drift into a daze. And long periods of flatlining can feel like spiritual death, or at least spiritual sleep, can't they? That's why oneness with God fades from our awareness. Our identity, purpose, and destiny get wrapped in haze.

And here's an even darker downside: Most of us are used to flatlining. In fact, we're so used to flatlining that we despise valleys. We want the highlands of spiritual vigor without the lowlands of spiritual strife. Of course, that's impossible. Peaks can't exist without valleys. If there are highlands, then there must be lowlands. But that doesn't keep our hearts from attempting to jump from peak to peak, from trying to live all of life in the highlands of passion, comfort, and joy.

How are you doing with this, by the way? Are you succeeding, or are you frustrated? The answer probably changes everyday, maybe even every hour. But one thing is obvious: This isn't sustainable. We can't go peak-jumping through life, not without experiencing a world of frustration.

But far more important than this, the valleys and lowlands are often the places where we're most open to spiritual growth, most attuned to the words of God, most humble to receive rebuke, most aware of the ceramic nature of spiritual life. In comfort, we're ossified and close-fisted. In suffering, we're wet and open-palmed. If we make peak-jumping the end-all of our spiritual lives, we'll not just end up frustrated and discouraged; we'll also end up immature, underdeveloped. Like unfledged birds, we'll lack the plumage we need to take flight and grow closer to the God of light, who illuminates the deepest valleys and smiles on the highest peaks.

But if we can't go peak-jumping, if we can't live in the highlands, what can we do? How do we keep the fully satisfying, life-giving oneness of God central? How do we really embrace the truth that God is living inside us and is calling for our constant communion?

The only other option is to keep moving up and down the terrain God sets before us. And, over time, we might find a way to embrace both directions. How? By finding a constant, something we can always grasp with the dry and dirty hands of hope. You can probably guess what it is. Throughout the book, I'm going to argue that this hope-giving constant can be represented more broadly by a number—*one*—and more narrowly by a person—*Jesus*. Hope, after all, "is a person, and his name is Jesus."[17]

In the broader sense, oneness is something Jesus talked about in his high priestly prayer, but we'll get to that in a few pages. In the narrower sense, the Apostle Paul offers the clearest reference.

> I rejoiced in the Lord greatly that now at length you have revived your concern for me. You were indeed concerned for me, but you had no opportunity. Not that I am speaking of being in need, for I have learned in whatever situation I am to be content. I know how to be brought low, and I know how to abound. In any and every circumstance, I have learned the secret of facing plenty and hunger, abundance and need. I can do all things through him who strengthens me. (Phil. 4:10–13)

Paul was a mountain climber. Like you. Like me. He scaled the lowlands of sorrow, shame, self-pity, loss, and terror—bobbing on the open ocean after shipwreck, cringing at the faces of Christians he'd persecuted, burying pride beneath the soil of mercy (then digging it up and reburying). Paul knew the depths. But he also knew the heights. He felt the Spirit push him up the hillsides of grace and gratitude. He vibrated his vocal cords in joy even behind the bars of a prison cell. He saw God's purpose for his life like a ray of sunshine burning through the fog. The light that once blinded him now went before him. And he found joy in it. Yes, Paul knew the heights.

But throughout all of his climbing, Paul found something else to focus on besides the terrain. He didn't ignore the terrain. None of us can. But neither did he set his face only to the dirt and dust. He lifted his chin to look up at his savior. And in that looking, he found a constant, his still point in a turning world, his straight path through any terrain. He found contentment in Christ. And as William Barcley put it, "Contentment comes not by finding conditions suitable to us but by God's fashioning our spirits to our conditions."[18] Spirit-fashioning—that's how we find contentment in Christ. (Were you hoping for a different answer?)

Now, how does God do that fashioning? Through the Spirit, in conformity to his Son (Rom. 8:9–17, 29; Phil. 11:6; Col. 3:3–10; 2 Cor. 3:18). Our ultimate contentment, then, is in God himself, especially in the person of Jesus Christ, to whom we are joined by the Spirit and are thus one with the Father. Contentment, in this sense, is not so much a general practice as it is a particular person. Though it sounds a bit like new age wisdom, you don't find contentment; he finds you. And then you carry him with you into the wild country of daily life (Matt. 28:20).

The more I read the Bible, the more obvious it becomes that Paul pocketed his Lord. He brought him everywhere—up to every summit and down to every depression. His contentment was found in an ever-present person. And because that person never leaves us, contentment doesn't either. At least, it doesn't have to. Just look at the atrocities Paul suffered in his life: stoning, shipwreck, ridicule, death threats. And he says, "I have learned in whatever situation I am to be content." That, my friends, is the fruit of a hundred seasons of hardship. That's the conclusion of a real mountain climber.

Spiritually speaking, if flatlining isn't an option, and if we can't go peak-jumping through life, then we're bound to be mountain climbers just as Paul was. And that means we need to learn the hard lesson of embracing both directions of spirituality: the descent of struggle and strife along with the ascent of hope and glory. We need both to make a whole heartbeat show up on the monitor.

But, as Paul did, we're also bound to find contentment in Christ, to carry him with us down every dusty road of the ordinary, right on through the gates of eternity. Where we go, Christ goes. Where Christ goes, we go. A person is our path. A person is our destination. A person is our ever-present guide. Our life isn't so much about *where* we're going as it is about *with* whom and *to* whom we're going.

You and I, we're mountain climbers on heart monitors. That's life on this side of paradise. But oneness with God is the good news that our heart monitors can stay grounded on something. Our hearts can beat strongly on Christ. Oneness with God is the good news that our path through tough terrain is already cut. Christ cut it. And in him we're one with the God who knows the way, the God who *is* the way!

We begin where we are. Right here. On this page. Oneness is ours. We take it up together.

Who and Where We Are, Again

Now, before we go barreling forward into the treasure trove of oneness with God and contentment in Christ, let's back up a moment and look at first things, at who we are in light of the God we profess to know and serve. Then we can see how the ideas of oneness and contentment in Christ are central to our identity, why we lose sight of them, and how we can keep ourselves, by the Spirit's grace, on the path of Christ.

Go back to identity with me. That palpitating, muscle-moving, conscious creature you see in the mirror each morning—*who* are you? Maybe even better: *what* are you? It may seem as if I'm wasting words, but if you don't fully embrace the answers that Scripture offers to these *who* and *what* questions, you'll be severely misguided in a thousand practical ways. These aren't abstract inquiries; they're concrete concerns.

For instance, if you define yourself on empirical grounds, as a collection of nerve cells, body tissue, and platelets all wrapped in skin and buttressed by bones, then you really don't have a reason to stop and say a kind word to the person making your latte at the local coffee shop. Sure, there's the "everyone should be a decent human being" argument, but that argument has no ultimate basis. Why are we supposed to be decent human beings, again? If your definition of what it means to be human is only empirical (i.e., we are physical beings who respond to stimuli all around us), you have no answers besides selfish ones (e.g., "what goes around comes around" or some other version of social karma). Your answers for all the *why* questions in life ultimately come back to you, because you is all that matters: your own satisfaction and fulfillment.

With Scripture, however, we get a God-focused answer (since everything in Scripture is God-focused), and the answer shapes every little thing we do. The answers are simple but often get lost on us, perhaps *because* they're so simple.

What are you? An image bearer of the Trinity.
Who are you? A person in Christ.

Why say a kind word to the neck-tattooed, disheveled barista struggling to snap the lid on your latte? Because you reflect the character of a kind, generous, thoughtful, compassionate, communion-loving God who called you out of death-dealing darkness and into life-giving light. Because you've been made new in the image of God's own Son (2 Cor. 5:17), and now you walk in the works your heavenly Father has prepared for you (Eph. 2:10), at the prodding of an ever-present Spirit (Rom. 8:9–16). There's a whole ocean of grace-infused purpose behind the order of a morning beverage. That is, if we carry with us a biblical view of who and what we are.

But we can be even more specific. After all, what does it really mean to bear God's image? A classic answer in Reformed theology is that we bear the image of God in our knowledge, righteousness, and holiness.[19] This is certainly true. But there's something deeper, something that runs beneath these God-honoring human behaviors. And Geerhardus Vos seems to have put his finger on it: "That man bears God's image means much more than that he is spirit and possesses understanding, will, etc. It means above all that he is disposed for communion with God, that all the capacities of his soul can act in a way that corresponds to their destiny only if they rest in God."[20] Being made in God's image means that we're always bent towards communion with him.

It's *God* that we want more than anything. He's the brilliant sun from which we've shot like rays through stardust.[21] And light must come to Light, illumination to Illuminator. Someway, somehow we must get through the darkness and see his face again, the face of God.

More than anything, we want an intimate relationship with our heavenly Father, our unbegotten light. He's the one who knows our beginning. He's the one who knows our ending. And he knows every chapter and verse in between. We want to know and be known, to love and be loved by the one who chose us before the foundation of the world (Eph. 1:4).

We want closeness with the Son, full of heavenly photons in his eternal begottenness, born into blood and bones to walk among us so that we might be restored to union with him (John 1:14; 17:21–22). He sees us as we are—with all the duplicity and waywardness and distraction and bravado—and still says, "Yes. I died for this one."

And we want to spread out our hands before the hearth of the Spirit. We want to feel the warmth of the flame who groans with us in our suffering and comforts us in our affliction (Rom. 8:26; John 14:26). We want to breathe with the Breath of God, to be caught up in the wind of his glory.

We want to be one with the Trinity. We want communion. Deep, unceasing, unflinching, unbreakable communion with the God who spoke us into motion. We want oneness with God. We yearn for it. That's where we started the book.

But I also assumed a problem at the start of this chapter: We don't *feel* it so often, do we? God himself promises that we *have* this, but we don't *feel* it. And because we don't feel it, we don't live from it or out of it. It's not the beam we set our feet on. We stand on weaker wood. We're barn swallows playing on rotten limbs.

We started this chapter by sensing our heart beat, by becoming more conscious of our physical and spiritual life and the daily terrain we traverse. It's time now to confess where we are. Why? Well,

> To confess is to free oneself, not only by admitting a sin or an omission but to profess a deeper allegiance, a greater dedication to something beyond the mere threat of immediate punishment or the desolation of being shunned. To confess is to declare oneself ready for a more courageous road.[22]

I want that road. And I want you to walk it with me. The first step is confession.

So, here's the confession: *We're out of touch.* Oneness with God feels like a rope covered in butter. We grab, and it slips. We grab, and it slips. The iteration breeds fatigue. We just can't seem to hold on to oneness with God. We're constantly overtaken by a thousand distractions or a plethora of idols (usually both). We'll get into the distractions in another chapter. But the result of all of them is that flatlining or peak-jumping we spoke about—the refusal to keep climbing terrain or the attempt to only seek the high points.

Being out of touch with God also means endlessly striving after wind, the absence of lasting contentment in Christ, and the search for contentment everywhere else. Our souls turn to stone. They warm in the light, cool in the darkness, but most often, they just sit, calloused and detached. Sometimes we even forget that oneness with God is possible. We forget that a rapturous and soul-piercing union with someone called Love can break through the clouded windows of momentary life with the hair-raising wind of the Spirit, invigorating and chilling our core. Oh, but it can! It can ... and it *will*.

And it's not just because we were made this way. It's also because God himself prayed for it. Our yearning for oneness wasn't just divinely implanted; it was also divinely petitioned. God sowed that seed of desire, but he also asked for water and light, sun and rain. He is the greatest gardener, after all. He planted the seed of oneness, but he also asked that our oneness be brought to full fruition. And when God (the Son) prays to God (the Father) in the power of God (the Spirit), there's no going back. No one can uproot the seed of oneness from the soil of the soul. No one. It's been beckoned and protected by the very speech of God, hemmed in by holy syllables.

Now, with this holy and divine desire for oneness, there's a pivotal purpose. And we'll get to that soon enough. In the remainder of the book, we'll be unpacking how this holy desire for oneness defines us, leads us, and calls us home. Here's the roadmap. We've already taken the first three steps.

- Yearning for Oneness
- What Is Oneness?
- Begin Where You Are
- The God of Oneness
- You Were Made for This
- The Absence of Oneness
- The Path to Oneness
- Oneness in Private
- Oneness in Public
- The Day Eternal

Throughout the book, there are discussion questions, prayers, and reader resources you can use to apply what you're learning. A book about something this deep is a waste if all you want is information, if all you're looking for is a "good read." In fact, I encourage you to read this book in a group setting, since dialogue and mutual prayer go hand-in-hand with the main theme of the book: latching on to the medium of language, which draws us into oneness with God.

Let's pray that God would move in our hearts so that we would treasure contentment in Christ and union with the Father, Son, and Spirit above all else. Is there really anything that can compare with it?

Reflection Questions and Prayer

1. How are you at mountain climbing? What do you tend to do in the valleys? What do you tend to do at the peaks?

2. What have been particular challenges for you in trying to find contentment in Christ? What other things in your life seem to take priority over your prayerful relationship with him?

3. Jesus Christ prayed for you! Read John 17:20–21 again. What do you think it means to be "one" with Jesus and the Father?

4. What's the purpose of our being one with God? Have a look at the end of John 17:21. What are some practical ways in which you think God might be sending you out to proclaim the gospel of Christ in your everyday life?

Prayer
Oh God of hope and glory,
Light unceasing,
I was made for oneness with you.

My separation from you is a tragedy,
And everyday I'm reminded of it.
But I'm also reminded of Christ.
In him, through the power of your Spirit,
I am one with you again.
I don't always feel as if I'm one with you,
But feelings are never final.
Draw me to gaze at you,
To fall in love with your character,
To dream of you,
My life-giving, self-sacrificing shepherd.
Help me to find a way today
To show others that this oneness
Is worth living and dying for,
That you're the most precious,
The most costly,
The most rapturous joy
We could ever find.
Thank you for bringing me
Into you.

Reader Resource: A Oneness Poem

I'm an open room for you.
Turn the handle. Enter, please.
There's nothing else I can do

But bow down on my tired knees
And ask for truth.

Countless wicks of thought are lit.
All around distractions burn.
Quell the flames as you see fit.
In the rising smoke I'll turn,
Face you, and sit.

You in me and me in you—
I want only to be close,
Bonding with the favored few,
Father, Son, and Holy Ghost,
Who make me new.

Lesser things grasp at my will
To pull me out the door again.
You quiet every noise and thrill,
Whispering our eternal when,
And make me still.

Chapter Four

THE GOD OF ONENESS

It's been my habit to write my books by hand. This morning, the candle on my tabletop flickers and waves in the blue light of dawn. The black wick inside the flame is bent forward like a giraffe's neck. An orange-red ember glows in the embrace of light. Silent. Strong. Illuminating. That is my candle.

> The wick is strong. The wick is still.
> It stands inside the flame.
> The flame can dance and turn at will,
> Ever-moving but the same.

All analogies, like children, can only run so far. They spring and leap and turn with wild energy before they search for a bench to rest on. That bench is *the mystery of truth*. An odd expression, isn't it? We live with the illusion that truth means the absence of mystery. We act as if truth is fact and mystery is fiction. But we're deeply confused. Truth is a person, as we noted earlier (John 14:6). A living, life-giving, self-sacrificing person. Truth is one who *loves* so fiercely that he breaks down death's door and lets the light of eternity burn through the black. Truth is the one who gives to others what they stole from him, who blesses when cursed and eases when insulted. Truth says "yes" to our "no." He whispers "enter" when we scream "exit!" And this great person of truth is before us, beyond us, beneath us, and beside us. He is even *inside* us. We are a home for another, who becomes our home. That was the treasure of John 14:23 we already looked at. Is this not the burning hearth of mystery, the star that calls our eyes out through the deep midnight of our own meaning? The mystery of truth—that's where all our analogies bow and rest.

Nowhere is this more obvious than with the Trinity, with God. So, when I think of God as the candle on my tabletop, I know that analogy will only go a few feet before needing a rest.[23] But they might be feet worth walking.

Our unbegotten Father is the wick. He knows no beginning. He always was, always is, and always will be. But he's never alone. The Son is the flame surrounding him, finding his amber glory in the relationship, the inseparability of wick and flame, the wonder of union. The Spirit is the heat that radiates into the room, wafting above the light, coursing around the wick. Wick, flame, and heat are one candle. The beauty lies in the relationship, the constant fellowship of the elements for a singular purpose: to bring light and warmth to a dark room.

Of course, the analogy breaks down quickly. It can only play for so long, like a child on the playground. I'm using the analogy so that a portrait of God might strike home with us. Analogies never communicate everything perfectly, but they do "communicate effectively."[24] The candle image is effective in showing us the unity and diversity of God, the oneness and relationship. This is who God is.

God is a communion of distinct and eternal persons, each loving and glorifying the others. If we're going to understand and embrace oneness with God, we have to start there.

As I mentioned earlier, we often grasp at oneness with God as a feeling, a visceral sense of peace that transcends description. But because it transcends description, we let it transcend identification, and then we don't even know what we're looking for. It's at that point that we substitute something else for oneness with God. But, as we'll see in the next chapter, this is tragic because oneness is precisely what we're made for. John Piper famously says, "God is most glorified in us when we are most satisfied in him." The "him" is the Trinity—Father, Son, and Spirit. We are most satisfied in *fellowship*, not in feelings.

In fact, feelings are always children of fellowship; they are attached to relationships and emerge from them. Chasing after feelings is like chasing after the steam of a hot meal. What we're really after is the food, not the steam that emanates from it. The same is true of God. We're after *him*, not the feelings that come from being in relationship to him.

To embrace this, we have to start by understanding the trinitarian nature of God. That's why theologians call the doctrine of the Trinity "the earmark" of Christianity.[25] It's foundational and fundamental. We have to start here.

The God of oneness is the God of communion, the God of relationship. We have to know this—not just conceptually but spiritually. It needs to become the greatest landmark on the landscape of our heart. We were made for the God of communion, the God of fellowship. Each one of us is one made for three. In fellowship with the Father, Son, and Spirit, we are set free like pigeons let out of a cage. The sky is our union with three holy persons. We flap and sing and soar *in* this God. We have our being *in* this holy family (Acts 17:28).

We need to embrace this in terms of God's *identity*. Yes—God *is* three persons, and "the persons are indeed distinct, but they are also profoundly one, through coinherence."[26] Coinherence is just a fancy way of saying that each person of the Godhead lives in the others. The Father and the Spirit live in the Son; the Son and Spirit live in the Father; the Father and Son live in the Spirit. They *abide* in one another. They are personal guests and homes at the same time. They can never be separated. They are an ultimate fellowship, sharing one essence. That's who God is, and we need to embrace it. Not understand it, but embrace it; lean into it, act on it as the bedrock of existence.

But we also need to grasp God's trinitarian unity in his *action*, in all that he does. "The actions of God in time . . . are always the actions of the one true God, who is three persons. And yet we can also see a differentiation in the *mode* in which each person acts in bringing about the major turning points in history."[27] Because the Father, Son, and Spirit live in each other, "we cannot *separate* the activities of the three persons," as if one was acting independently of the others.[28]

Why do we need to know this about the actions of God? Because we have a tendency of breaking up the Godhead, of separating the persons. And because doing this is false, it harms our relationship with the God of oneness. As Timothy Jennings wrote, "Love cannot flow where lies about God abound."[29]

Let me give you the most common example. Have you ever been taught that God the Father, because he's so holy, is constantly frowning at sinners, that he's angry, wrathful, and bent on punishment? Of course, he *is* holy and righteous and shows holy wrath at places throughout Scripture, as he alone has the right to do. And yet, if we cling to this portrait of the Father in isolation from what the rest of Scripture says about him, how do we look at the Son? As the one who appeased the wrath of God. The Father was bent on punishing us until Jesus came along and took our punishment on himself. Thank goodness the Son could calm the Father down! We would have been obliterated. And the Spirit, we think, tries to keep us holy after we believe in Jesus so that the Father doesn't flip his lid again.

Doesn't this sound as if Jesus and the Spirit are trying to hold back the Father, as if the Father were the angry playground kid you just tripped?

Now, it's true that sin needs atonement, that God is holy, that he punishes the wicked, that he hates sin. Scripture testifies to all of those things. We all know Isaiah 53 and the suffering servant who "bore our iniquities," who took on the punishment that we deserved so that we might be saved. And we know also that the Spirit empowers us in our daily walk to make us holy. So, what's the problem?

The problem is that we're separating the action of God and treating the divine persons as if they have three separate wills. The Father wants to punish, the Son wants to save, and the Spirit just wants to help. This portrait of the Godhead is false because it separates what *cannot* be separated. It tears apart the action and will of God and divvies up the pieces among the persons. But God is one, and has *one* will. The three persons live in one another and share that one will. It's not that God the Father wants to punish while the Son wants to appease him and the Spirit just wants to help us out. There are no warring wills in God. There is one will shared by the persons, and that will is to seek and save the lost, to enlarge the holy family, to fill the house of God with the people of God. The Father wants that. The Son wants that. The Spirit wants that. There are no warring wills.

Think of it more like sin as a disease and the Trinity as the physician. The Father plans the treatment; the Son carries out the procedure; and the Spirit focuses on our long-term recovery. But even in this analogy, there's more beautiful mystery than meets the eyes.[30]

While the Father plans, the Son and Spirit are *in* him, participating in that planning. While the Son carries out the procedure—in his incarnation, life, death, and resurrection—the Father and the Spirit are *in* him, participating in the procedure. And while the Spirit works constantly on our long-term recovery, the Father and Son are *in* him, participating in that recovery. They are one. They live in one another. Each person is *always* participating in the acts of the one God.

Note that I say "participate" here to allow for mystery. This is the teaching of *divine appropriations*.[31] There are certain acts that are more *appropriate* to one person, even while the other persons are somehow acting. Jesus died on the cross, not the Father or the Spirit. It was the Spirit who was poured out at Pentecost, not the Father or the Son. Certain actions are most appropriate to one of the divine persons, but there is mystery in how the other persons are involved. I don't pretend to understand this. It's beyond my creaturely pay grade. But I have to affirm it as the truth because that's what Scripture teaches.

And here's a fringe benefit: I don't live as if God is at war with himself over me. Surely, no Christian would say this, but we *act* like it. We act like the Father is the angry kid on the playground, wearing a white track suit and just waiting for one of the toddlers to flick a piece of mulch at him. And when we flick it (as we're so prone to do, beyond all reason), we huddle behind the Son and Spirit. "Please, don't let him smite me!"

Let's drop the playground portrait. Really. Let's let it go. It's not true. God is more like the kind teacher who's always making rounds and helping those in need—catching us when we fall off the bars and cleaning us up when we nose-dive into the dirt. The Father, Son, and Spirit love us. The Father, Son, and Spirit desire our salvation, our trust, our redemption. The Father, Son, and Spirit want us to make them our home, and they want us to be their home (John 14:23).

The God of oneness wants *our* fellowship, *our* company. That's the unbelievable good news of the gospel. What God has always wanted, God has done. What we have always longed for has been given. We find great joy and peace in that when we embrace the trinitarian identity and action of God, who has always been *for* us. Doesn't that make you feel more at peace when running through the playground of life? Go on: swing a little higher. God—all of him—is right there, right *here*.

Back to the Nature of God

Now that we're clear on God being one in both his being and his actions, we're in a better place to understand what oneness with him means. Let's explore this a bit more in terms of God's nature before we draw out implications for who we are in the next chapter.

Since we've had some discussion already, would you be able to answer a *big* question? It's actually the biggest question we can ask, and we need to have the answer ready at hand for every spiritual problem and theological quandary. Here it is: *Who is God?*

If you pause, that's okay. It's not a question we can answer without some measure of silence. And the fact that we try to jump over silence is a shame, really. "Silence allows the silt to settle so we can see what gleams and swims below the surface."[32] What is it that swims below the surface? Curiosities. Wonders. Hopes. When all the silt settles, we just want to know who put us here and if he stays, if he still speaks, if we can speak back to him. We want to know *him*, not just know *of* him.

One of my favorite theologians put it simply. "The Bible begins with the account that God created man after His own image and likeness, in order that he should know God his Creator aright, should love Him with all his heart, and should live with Him in eternal blessedness."[33] In order that he should know God—we were created to *know* him. We were custom-made for a divine-human relationship based on knowledge that God himself would give us.

The obvious follow-up question is, What do we know about him? You might say that this very question is at the heart of Scripture, smiling behind the shadows of the words. Ultimately, it's what all the details are about—the narratives and genealogies, the poems and prayers, the songs and the sayings. Scripture is a book about who God is and what he's done.

Because this is a book about oneness with God, I'm going to focus there: God's oneness and unity. That may seem impersonal on the surface. Don't we want to know much more about God than his "oneness"? Well, this oneness is actually the furthest thing from being impersonal. It's the most personal. In fact, it's the very thing that makes everything else personal. For God, oneness is not merely a thing (though God is surely one in essence); it is a portrait of intimate communion among Father, Son, and Spirit. Persons in deep, abiding communion—that's oneness for God. And it's that very truth that ensures the rest of our world is "shot through with personality."[34]

When we look at the world and the works of God in it, we witness this unique oneness of God, a harmony of unity (essence) and diversity (persons). That's why Bavinck writes,

> The unity and diversity in the works of God proceeds from and returns to the unity and diversity which exist in the Divine Being. That Being is one being, single and simple. At the same time that being is threefold in His person, in His revelation, and in His influence. . . . Therefore the article of the holy trinity is the heart and core of our confession, the differentiating earmark of our religion, and the praise and comfort of all true believers of Christ.[35]

"The differentiating earmark"—I love that. Trinitarian oneness, unity in diversity, is the thing that marks the uniqueness of our religion. It's the burning star in the sky of our faith. And we'll see later why it's the "praise and comfort of all true believers."

Bavinck's words do little more than reverberate biblical truth (as all good theology should). In Scripture, God tells his image-bearing creatures both that he is one (Deut. 6:4) and that he is three (Matt. 28:19).[36] He is, in other words, three-in-one.

You might be wondering why I'm harping on this. Why the sudden focus on theological doctrine? Because it has everything to do with what it means for us to be one with God. God's oneness comes with an invitation for communion because God *is* a communion of divine persons. This is often what it means when theologians say that God is *relational*.

The relational nature of God, the warm hearth of personal communion and fellowship, is the blue flame burning beneath our human fellowship with each other. As my friend and former teacher notes,

> Within God, the persons—the Father, the Son, and the Holy Spirit—have rich personal relations with one another. We are made like God, and that is why we can enjoy personal relationships. When we relate to one another, we rely on resources and powers that find their origin in God.[37]

Don't miss those words. "We rely on resources and powers that find their origin in God." Humans are leaning creatures. We must rest on God, leaning up against who he is, to do anything in this world, even to utter hello to a friend in the morning.

And I want also to focus on this uttering, this speech, for a moment. Speech is not just something we do. It's an intimate reflection of who we are and who God is. That's why in a previous chapter I called speech *communion behavior*.[38] Speech is at the heart of relationship, and relationship is at the heart of God.

This isn't just a poetic rant from an English major who wants everyone to appreciate the depth and beauty of language (true as that is). This is a New Testament teaching.

> The New Testament indicates that the persons of the Trinity speak to one another and enjoy profound personal relations with one another. These relationships within God show us the ultimate foundation for thinking about human personal relationships. God establishes a personal relationship with us, but, in addition, the persons of the Trinity have personal relations to one another. Personal relationships exist not solely among human beings, but also in divine-human relationships, and even in divine-divine relationships.[39]

Pause with me. Give yourself a few moments of silence. Let the silt settle. This is the truth swimming beneath the surface of our crazed and turning world. When the muck and the mud have settled, this is what we see. It's the answer to that question, Who is God?

God has the deepest of personal relationships in himself. In one sense, we can even say that God *is* a relationship. That's profoundly personal, isn't it? We're not dealing with a generic or abstract deity when it comes to the God of the Bible. We're dealing with the source of intimacy and communion. This is perhaps easiest for us to grasp when we think about God being communicative, a being who speaks. As one theologian wrote, "there is—and has been from all eternity—talk, sharing and communication in the innermost life of God. The true God is not silent; He talks."[40]

Being one with this sort of God means that communication will always be primary because love is always primary. Love is a relational behavior interwoven with communication. We can't be one with God when we don't speak with him and when we don't hear him speaking to us. We'll get into this later in the book when I present the concept of having a *speechpath* with God each day (an open line of daily communication).

Love requires a living relationship. It requires giving and taking, sharing and receiving. Many of us would have a far stronger relationship with God if we implemented that basic truth throughout each day. Communication with the God who speaks is not a fringe benefit of the Christian life; it's the core.

Theologians throughout Christian history have always known and treasured this truth. It's the gold coin pressed into every Christian's palm—the currency of communion.[41] Recent works of the last twenty to thirty years have brought it to the surface once again.[42] But note this: We should prioritize communication with God not just because it results in our spiritual growth, but because loving communication is central to the character and identity of God himself. As Michael Reeves put it, God is "the Father, loving and giving life to his Son in the fellowship of the Spirit. A God who is in himself love, who before all things could 'never be anything but love.' Having such a God happily changes everything."[43] Indeed. It does change everything.

A Oneness of Fellowship

The fact that God is three-in-one and communicates with himself in an eternal union of divine love means that oneness with him has certain qualities.

When we become one with God, we're not absorbed like a raindrop in a proverbial ocean of being. We don't dissolve and disappear. Oneness with God doesn't eclipse our personhood, just as the oneness of God's being doesn't eclipse the personhood of the Father, Son, and Spirit. When we talk about oneness with God, we're talking about a oneness of *fellowship*. I introduced this earlier, but we need to dig into this more deeply. What exactly does a oneness of fellowship mean? Here are three points that will help us wrap our minds around it.

1. A oneness of fellowship requires distinction. You can't talk about the "fellowship" of raindrops in an ocean. The ocean is an undifferentiated mass of liquid.[44] For fellowship to hold, there has to be distinctness. We can talk about Christian fellowship with our brothers and sisters precisely because we're *not* our brothers and sisters. We're distinct, and yet that distinctness doesn't threaten the unity of love that binds us in the Spirit of Christ. In fact, it's the opposite: our uniqueness as creatures made in God's image enhances and beautifies the communion we have with each other and with God. The richness of our fellowship lies in the harmony of unity and diversity. Such unity and diversity is actually rooted in the very nature of God, which makes perfect sense: we can't possess, enjoy, or reflect anything good that doesn't have its origin in him.[45]

2. A oneness of fellowship means unparalleled intimacy. God is intimate in himself, in ways we can't even fathom. In speaking of the Father, Son, and Spirit, Abraham Kuyper once put it this way:

> The Love-life whereby these Three mutually love each other is the Eternal Being Himself. This alone is the true and real life of love. The entire Scripture teaches that nothing is more precious and glorious than the Love of the Father for the Son, and of the Son for the Father, of the Holy Spirit for both. . . . Before God created heaven and earth with all their inhabitants, the eternal Love of Father, Son, and Holy Spirit shone with unseen splendor in the divine Being.[46]

A river of love runs bottomless in God. We cannot speak of its depth. And yet, while we can't ever comprehend this, God tells us we've been invited in. We've been called into the river of love.

There are many implications of this mysterious truth, but one that we'll revisit throughout this book is the need for dialogue. You cannot be intimate without mutual communication. There is no love without dialogue or expressive giving of some kind. Now, on God's part the giving is lopsided. He's poured out the inkwell of his thought and life on the pages of history and pressed down in Scripture all that we need to know about him. It reminds me of those stanzas from Frederick Lehman's hymn "The Love of God":

> Could we with ink the ocean fill,
> and were the skies of parchment made;
> were ev'ry stalk on earth a quill,
> and ev'ryone a scribe by trade;
> to write the love of God above
> would drain the ocean dry;
> nor could the scroll contain the whole,
> though stretched from sky to sky.

God is a giver, and his self-revelation is the greatest gift. It's always before us.

The question is, Are we giving ourselves to him? The simplest way to give ourselves to God is through prayer, the unrestrained outflow of our souls. Everything—the beauty and the blindness, the passion and the pain, the sweetness and the swill. We may not even have words to pray. That's okay. Groans are accepted and interpreted by God's Spirit (Rom. 8:26). But we have to talk. We have to share. We have to express. Without dialogue, oneness of fellowship wanes.

3. A oneness of fellowship means that we're bound for the home of God. And that, my friends, is eternity. I know it seems too good to be true, like the shadow of a childhood dream. But it's repeated all throughout Scripture. Our dwelling will be with God. There is nothing and no one who can push us off the road leading to our heavenly homestead. We're going there—regardless of how we feel or what we think. Once we have trusted Christ as savior, our room is prepared (John 14:2). I can't wait to see the bedding.

Now that we have a sense of what this oneness of fellowship entails, we're ready to begin looking at God's own prayer for us. This will set the tone for the chapters ahead, and we'll revisit it frequently.

Reflection Questions and Prayer

1. What are some of the ways in which God's truth is mysterious to you? Why is a particular truth comforting or frustrating?

2. How has the doctrine of the Trinity had an impact on your faith? Why do you think it's important to understand God as three persons in one essence?

3. If communication is central to God and to our relationship with him, what happens to us when we stop communicating with God in prayer and Scripture reading?

4. What are some ways in which the "oneness of fellowship with God" is threatened in your own life? What idols seek to take the place of God for you?

5. How do you think oneness with God is related to your

daily activities? Be creative.

Prayer
God, you've told us who you are.
You are three-in-one, a holy family.
Your love is a river I've been invited into.
I'm often unaware of the water.
I even resist the current at times;
I chase after other things.
Help me to know deep in my being
That you are my home and that I am yours,
That fellowship with you is my purpose,
That fellowship with you is my destiny.
Help me to speak to you about my joys and passions,
My frustrations and disappointments,
My ambitions and my soul's yearning.
Spirit, remind me constantly that you are listening.

Reader Resource: Our Calling as Listeners

Though in this chapter I have talked about the importance of speaking with God, it's critical to remember that we were created to be *listeners*. Adam McHugh's book *The Listening Life* has been immensely helpful to me, and I highly recommend it.[47] For now, here are some ways in which we need to develop as listeners. In which area do you feel you need the most work?

- **Listening to Scripture.** Reading God's word isn't just a matter of processing marks on a page, of comprehending narratives or laments or poems. Reading is an act of listening. Listening means giving your undivided attention to another person's message and the accompanying action it may call for. Since God is the author of Scripture, when we read it, we're trying to listen for his message to us in both *meaning* and *application*. We can *hear* something and understand it without *listening*. Listening implies devotion and obedience. Hearing says, "I acknowledge what you're saying." Listening says, "I'm devoted to doing what you're calling me to do." We all need to work on *listening* to God's word, not just hearing it.

- **Listening to Creation.** God speaks through the created world about his nature (Rom. 1:20; Ps. 19:1–4). We can't truly or reliably understand what he's saying about himself apart from Scripture (we go through special revelation to interpret general revelation), since we need redeemed hearts and minds to interpret the world around us. Yet, God is still speaking about himself in creation. Are you in the practice of examining something in creation and asking, "God, what are you saying about yourself through *this*?" In other words, have you been listening to God's world?

- **Listening to Others.** We're usually aware of our need for improvement here. Everyone needs to be better at really listening to someone else's words and not just waiting for a turn to speak. Listening doesn't mean we try to think up an answer or response while someone is speaking to us. It means we empathize quietly and soak in someone else's perspective, someone's view of the world. We don't enter conversations so that we can solve problems (as tempting as that is); we enter conversations to commune with other human beings, to let them share themselves with us, to gain new perspective from those who see and experience life differently from us. How are you at listening to other people? If you find yourself itching for your turn to speak, you probably need a lot of work. And we're all in that position sometimes.

- **Listening to Your Pain.** Our pain and suffering has something to say to us, something to teach us. Suffering isn't in our life to tear us apart; it's there to conform us to the glorious image of Jesus Christ, in all of his beautiful complexity. Instead of focusing all of our attention on how we feel and why we're feeling a certain way, what if we focused on Christ-conformity questions? God, how are you trying to shape me to Christ through this pain? What element of his character do you want me to see? There's always an answer.

Chapter Five

THE PRAYER OF PRAYERS

Much of the book up to this point has really been preparing us to read one of the greatest prayers in Scripture. The greatest prayers are the purest, most potent, and most efficacious. They don't wander into the presence of God like a weak smoke trail; they cut through the darkness of doubt. They blaze. They burn—hot and holy—into the throneroom of the almighty. The angels stare and marvel in their winged worship. "What is this?" they say. "Clean words of hope for the God who sees."

In fact, that image isn't elevated enough. Strong and bright are the prayerful words of a holy person in the presence of God. But what about the words of God himself? What happens when God speaks to God? Darkness spreads like silent ink. Stars blaze. Gravity hugs turning spheres into family circles. Water ripples and roams. Color and light sing their ancient song in waves of energy. Life rests on bones and dresses in muscle and skin. Breath begets movement. Creation happens.

And after God's choral poem of creation was marred by sin, its stanzas kicked and couplets crushed, still God speaks to God.[48] He redeems with his mouth. All throughout history, he speaks his word to guide the world. Eventually, he even speaks his Word from *before* the world (John 17:5). And what happens? What happens when the eternal Word of God pushes his way into the world? Crooked limbs straighten (John 5:1–8). Cracked and scaling skin smoothes over (Matt. 8:1–4). The locked doors of broken eyes fall open (Acts 9:1–19). Empty lungs fill with breath again, and the dead come back from their silent sleep (John 11:38–44). Living water begets living souls. Re-creation happens.

When God speaks to God, things happen, things no one can thwart, things no one can imagine. When God speaks to God, change courses into dry valleys on the riverbeds of promise. And that's exactly what we have in John 17, the Prayer of Prayers. This is God (Jesus) speaking to God (the Father) in the power of God (the Spirit). We may have trouble believing that we can be one with God. But we need to hear God himself talk about it. John 17 is going to be our diamond for this book. We're going to gaze at it. We're going to let the prism of this passage refract light on our souls all across the color spectrum. It's going to be beautiful. And change is going to happen. It *must*. That's what happens when God speaks to God.

Are you in? If you are, then read this slowly. Read it prayerfully. Read it many times over. These are words for your soul.

When Jesus had spoken these words, he lifted up his eyes to heaven, and said, "Father, the hour has come; glorify your Son that the Son may glorify you, ² since you have given him authority over all flesh, to give eternal life to all whom you have given him. ³ And this is eternal life, that they know you, the only true God, and Jesus Christ whom you have sent. ⁴ I glorified you on earth, having accomplished the work that you gave me to do. ⁵ And now, Father, glorify me in your own presence with the glory that I had with you before the world existed. ⁶ I have manifested your name to the people whom you gave me out of the world. Yours they were, and you gave them to me, and they have kept your word. ⁷ Now they know that everything that you have given me is from you. ⁸ For I have given them the words that you gave me, and they have received them and have come to know in truth that I came from you; and they have believed that you sent me. ⁹ I am praying for them. I am not praying for the world but for those whom you have given me, for they are yours. ¹⁰ All mine are yours, and yours are mine, and I am glorified in them. ¹¹ And I am no longer in the world, but they are in the world, and I am coming to you. Holy Father, keep them in your name, which you have given me, that they may be one, even as we are one. ¹² While

I was with them, I kept them in your name, which you have given me. I have guarded them, and not one of them has been lost except the son of destruction, that the Scripture might be fulfilled. ¹³ But now I am coming to you, and these things I speak in the world, that they may have my joy fulfilled in themselves. ¹⁴ I have given them your word, and the world has hated them because they are not of the world, just as I am not of the world. ¹⁵ I do not ask that you take them out of the world, but that you keep them from the evil one. ¹⁶ They are not of the world, just as I am not of the world. ¹⁷ Sanctify them in the truth; your word is truth. ¹⁸ As you sent me into the world, so I have sent them into the world. ¹⁹ And for their sake I consecrate myself, that they also may be sanctified in truth. ²⁰ I do not ask for these only, but also for those who will believe in me through their word, ²¹ that they may all be one, just as you, Father, are in me, and I in you, that they also may be in us, so that the world may believe that you have sent me. ²² The glory that you have given me I have given to them, that they may be one even as we are one, ²³ I in them and you in me, that they may become perfectly one, so that the world may know that you sent me and loved them even as you loved me. ²⁴ Father, I desire that they also, whom you have given me, may be with me where I am, to see my glory that you have given me because you loved me before the foundation of the world. ^{25} O righteous Father, even though the world does not know you, I know you, and these know that you have sent me. ^{26} I made known to them your name, and I will continue to make it known, that the love with which you have loved me may be in them, and I in them."

There's a continent of truth here. A continent. My God . . . the prayer of the Son of God to his Father, using the very breath that gave the world its life; the longing for oneness with sinners and sellouts; the beauty of a divine person sent as a letter to a world constantly ignoring divine correspondence . . . it's almost too much.

We'll take the pages that follow to start trekking through the wild country of this continent, and we'll barely make it past the coast. But for now, know that in this precious prayer God himself prayed for you. What did he ask for? He asked for *oneness* (17:11, 21–23). God wants oneness with you. God (in Jesus Christ) prayed to God (the Father) through the power of God (the Spirit) for *this*.

Let that soak in for a few minutes. If you think oneness with God is a cloudy abstraction without the fingers to grip our personal lives, think again. *God* asked for this. This is the desire of his heart. Can we really afford to not make his desire our desire? Isn't this the most important thing in the world? Mustn't this be something not just worth living for, but worth dying for? More than that! Worth being raised from the dead for?! Oh my friend, wrap your arms around this passage and embrace. Just hold it for a while. Just stay here with me.

The Oneness Jesus Asks for

Start with something basic: What we've talked about as a *oneness of fellowship* is something that *God* wants for us. It's not just something we long for; it's something that God wills. That's precisely why Jesus prays for it in John 17. In this passage, the Son of God is asking God the Father for oneness with us in the power of God the Spirit. God is praying to God by the power of God for this one thing. If that doesn't blow your mind, I don't know what will.

But what exactly does Jesus mean when he asks for us to be "one" with him and the Father (and, by necessary extension, the Spirit)?

We can begin answering that question by focusing on a few verses, but it's essential that we understand this plea for oneness in context. That context is a *witnessing* context. In John 17:8, Jesus says, "For I have given them the words that you gave me, and they have received them and have come to know in truth that I came from you; and they have believed that you sent me." Believing that Jesus has been sent by God is a recurring motif in John's Gospel. In verse 18, Jesus confirms that he is sending the disciples into the world just as he was sent. Then in verse 20 he focuses on "those who will believe in me through their word" (that's you and me), which again is given in the context of *witnessing* to what God has done in sending the Son. And again in verses 21 and 23, Jesus prays for this oneness "so that the world may believe that you have sent me" and "so that the world may know that you sent me and loved them even as you loved me." Clearly, our oneness with God is a missional light. Though our oneness with God has eternity in store for us, while we're walking this earth, that oneness has a missional purpose. Our oneness with God is meant to be a testimony, burning and drawing others to gaze up and grasp at the God of communion.

Within this missional context, what exactly does it mean for us to be "one" with God? The verses that demand our attention are the following.

- 17:11, "And I am no longer in the world, but they are in the world, and I am coming to you. Holy Father, keep them in your name, which you have given me, that they may be one, even as we are one."

- 17:21, "that they may all be one, just as you, Father, are in me, and I in you, that they also may be in us, so that the world may believe that you have sent me."

- 17:22, "The glory that you have given me I have given to them, that they may be one even as we are one"

- 17:23, "I in them and you in me, that they may become perfectly one, so that the world may know that you sent me and loved them even as you loved me."

Let's start by nodding with Andreas Köstenberger: "Such unity is beyond human ability and is the result and gift of divine grace."[49] We can't get this oneness or unity for ourselves. It doesn't come from human grasping; it comes from divine giving.

But what does John (and Jesus) mean more specifically? The Greek word John uses is *eis*, meaning one "in contrast to the parts, of which a whole is made up."[50] In other words, we are not talking about an undifferentiated mass. This isn't ocean water oneness. It's a oneness of distinct persons that make up a community, or a communion of persons. And Jesus is clear that there is a hierarchy at play here.

"The unity between Son and Father will serve as the foundation and wellspring for the unity among believers; this, in turn, will make it possible for the world . . . to see through and beyond the mission of believers to the one who sent them (Jesus), just as Jesus's contemporaries were enabled to see past Jesus to the one who sent him, God the Father."[51] Richard Baukham echoes the same truth:

> The general sense (not precisely stated, as is typical of Johannine discourse) is that from the loving communion between the Father and the Son flows the love with which Jesus loved his disciples, a love that enables them to enjoy an intimate, "in-one-another" relationship with Jesus and his Father, and it is from this overflowing of divine love into the world that the oneness of believers among themselves stems.[52]

Our oneness with God and with each other is based upon the oneness of the Father and Son (and Spirit, though John does not emphasize that point here). That's to say, our oneness with God has a foundation: a oneness of love rooted in God himself. Remember that the oneness we are called into is a *oneness of fellowship*. This truth provoked Herman Ridderbos to write that our goal as believers is not some sort of abstract unity,

> but 'unity in us,' being one 'as we are one,' where 'even as' not only indicates resemblance between the church's unity and the unity between the Father and the Son, but also gives the church's unity its ground and character. Accordingly, the theme of this passage can only be 'that they may all be one in us.'[53]

We are dealing here with an overwhelmingly personal unity, an *in-us* unity where "us" refers to the Father, Son, and Spirit.

In this unity, we don't lose our distinctness. Again, this is based on the truth that the Father and Son don't lose their distinctness in light of their unity. In our distinctness, we are "to be one in purpose, in love, in action undertaken with and for one another, in joint submission to the revelation received."[54] Christians are to be "so identified with God and dependent upon him for life and fruitfulness, that they themselves become the locus of the Father's life and work in them."[55]

This is a lot to take in. Let's not rush to run through a holy torrent of truth.

Begin with the first component: the unity of the persons in the Trinity. The oneness of the Father, Son, and Spirit in love, power, and joy burns brighter than a thousand suns... in eternity. There's no such thing as a time when this was not. This is infinite oneness with unparalleled intimacy. And as humans on this side of paradise, we simply can't fathom it. It's beyond us. That doesn't mean we should bypass it. Quite the contrary: this should be the impetus for passionate worship. More than anything else, we want to be known and loved. Yet here is the God who intimately knows and loves himself from all eternity: the hearth of holiness and the wellspring of joyous communion. Praise God for being who he is!

> The love I need is yours already,
> My Father, Son, and Holy Ghost.
> Guide my steps and keep me steady
> Since you are the oneness I want most.

The second component of this rapturous, divinely rooted unity is that we can be one with this God and with each other. Our oneness rests on a divine building block that can't crack or corrode. We can trust in our oneness with God and with each other because *God* is beneath it all.

And our oneness is brought under a name.[56] This may seem less important. Isn't the oneness in focus here? Yes, but just as the oneness has a missional purpose (to spread the good news that God sent his Son into the world), it also has an identifying marker: the name of God. Here's Herman Ridderbos again,

> What constitutes and qualifies this unity of the coming community and its incorporation into the fellowship of the Father and the Son is its having been brought and kept under the rule of the word and name of God, which the Father has given to his Son, and the Son has revealed to his own (vss. 6–8, 11–12).[57]

The name of God—given to the Son and revealed to God's people—is no mere sequence of sounds. It is the fortress of their union. It is the place where God's people gather and stand in power, united to their maker and their members. Where once in Babel we strove to lift up our own names and became dispersed, now in Christ we strive to lift up God's name and grow together. Our oneness with God—built upon the sure foundation of oneness among the Father, Son, and Spirit—is the answer to the three questions posed in the subtitle of this book.

That, I believe, is why "Jesus's concern for his followers' unity is his greatest burden as his earthly mission draws to a close."[58] Our oneness with God is not a fairytale fancy. It's not something to store in the greenhouse of our daydreams. It's the beating heart of our existence, thudding to a rhythm that has no end. We are mountain climbers (recall the earlier analogy) because oneness is in our bones, and it's at the top of the tallest mountain. With every step into the rocky earth of adversity, we push upward towards our eternal destiny of oneness. As I mentioned in a previous chapter, our call as Christians is clear and simple: further up and further in (Lewis, *The Last Battle*).

We were *made* for this oneness. That's why we yearn for it in ways that bleed beyond words. That's why Jesus prayed for this. We were made for oneness with the God who is one with himself. And if Jesus has prayed for this, if God speaks to God about it, then it's going to happen for his people.

Before walking down the biblical path to that oneness, let's spend some more pages looking at this truth—that we were *made* for oneness with God. If we start there, we'll begin to understand why we're missing oneness in our everyday lives and how it can be restored by the Spirit of God drawing us deeper into Christ.

Reflection Questions and Prayer

1. Have you ever thought about the truth that God prays to God in John 17? What does this reveal about God's role in the work of redemption?

2. Why is there a "missional" context for our oneness with God?

3. In your own words, what would you say it means to be "one" with God in the sense Jesus is discussing in John 17?

4. Why might Christians struggle to be inspired by what Jesus prays for in John 17?

Prayer

God of oneness, you prayed for me.
You prayed that I would be one with you
So that the world might see your glory.
Convince my stubborn heart
To believe what seems unbelievable.
Teach me more about yourself
So that I can go deeper in union with you.
Thank you for being the foundation
Of our oneness with you and with each other
In the Spirit.
When sin threatens that oneness,
Help us to see it and strike it down.
Help us to guard our oneness with you
So that the watching world might more clearly perceive
The beauty of what you've done.

Reader Resource: What Makes Communion?

John Owen famously wrote,

> Our communion . . . with God consists in his *communication of himself unto us, with our return unto him* of that which he requires and accepts, flowing from that *union* which in Jesus Christ we have with him. And it is twofold: (1) *perfect and complete*, in

the full fruition of his glory and total giving up of ourselves to him, resting in him as our utmost end; which we shall enjoy when we see him as he is; and (2) *initial and incomplete*, in the firstfruits and dawnings of that perfection which we have here in grace.[59]

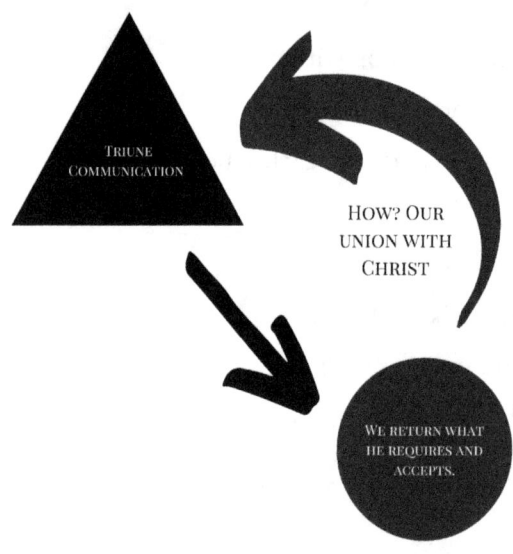

There is a call from God and a requirement of our response, but this can only happen through our union with Christ. So, when Jesus prays for oneness with us in John 17, he's aware that this oneness cannot come apart from him. Jesus is the bridge.

And if we believe in Christ, then we *have* him. And yet, there's that troubling part of Owen's definition: "initial and incomplete." We feel that incompleteness, don't we? Things constantly get in the way of our perfect communion with God, our oneness of fellowship with the Trinity. The question is, what are they?

We each need to answer that question for ourselves, but there are some universals out there. When we don't give God what he "requires and accepts," then we can't be perfectly one with him. Holiness doesn't keep dirty house guests. On this side of paradise, we fall into habits of embracing what God doesn't require (e.g., money, professional ambition and success, sexual fulfillment) and offering what he won't accept (half-hearted commitment, rebellion, selfishness, egoism disguised as humility). A large part of the Christian life is praying for and watching the Holy Spirit refine us into the image of Christ by unharnessing our stubborn will from what God doesn't require or accept, turning us in a new direction. But it's a long process.

Until we're at God's side in eternity, we need to ask the Spirit to train our hearts. We need training to identify what God doesn't require or accept, and then we need God-given will power to turn away from those things and choose the path of the Spirit. The good news is that, as the Spirit works in us to turn us away from sin and to help us chase after the things of God's own heart, we develop a *holy habit*. The beautiful things of the self-giving God, the one who gave all of himself to us in Christ, start to germinate in us. As John Mark Comer writes,

> Every time you sow to the Spirit and invest the resources of your mind and body into nurturing your inner man or woman's connection to the Spirit of

God, you plant something deep in the humus of your central fulcrum, which, over time, takes root and bears the fruit of a Christlike character.[60]

The fruit of Christlikeness comes through the Spirit cultivating a holy habit in us, a habit of choosing God over the world. And a holy habit is harder to break than a fluttering will, always chasing after the things we don't need or the things God won't accept.

What I'm saying is that communion with God, our oneness with him, is experienced little by little. Our growth in holiness often comes in tiny decisions, not momentous events. But that's exciting when you think about it, because that means you have an opportunity to experience greater depths of oneness with God *right now*. Your decision to make dinner for your family, to encourage your spouse without being asked, to pick up the crushed Pepsi bottle on the side of the road—these tiny decisions are woven into the path of your oneness with God. Oneness with God, then, isn't a general abstraction too far from practicality to fathom. Instead, it's a colossal truth leading up the slope of God's great mountain. At this very moment, you could be going further up and further in. You could be taking a tiny step up Jacob's ladder. It's all a matter of asking the Spirit to empower you in the little moments.

Chapter Six

YOU WERE MADE FOR THIS

We've now seen who God is in relation to oneness and how Jesus asks for this oneness with us in the Prayer of Prayers. In this chapter, we slow down to examine a certain *order* to the oneness we experience. But I want to open by reminding us once more that oneness with God—communion with him—is what we were made for. Though I've discussed this in other chapters, it needs repetition. Deep truths like this need to be etched into us because there are so many counterfeits we run after, so many false destinies we chase. Let's start with another etching.

Made for Oneness

The moon is a thumbnail in the sky this morning, silent and staring. It's as if the whole atmosphere were made for this moment and his crescent smile.

There's a snippet of a Robert Browning poem that's carved out a stone home in the rock of my memory.

> Round the cape of a sudden came the sea,
> And the sun looked over the mountain's rim:
> And straight was a path of gold for him,
> And the need of a world of men for me.

The sun seems made for golden paths, just as the thumbnail moon this morning seems made for the blushing sunrise. Buried deep within things are the divine purposes for them; everything is made for something. Robert Browning, like the rest of us, was made for communion, for oneness. That's why he says "the need of a world of men for me." We are built to need others. We are built for the God of fellowship, the God who also surrounded us with fellow creatures. It's as clear as the moonlight this morning and the sun's coming gold: we are made for communion.

Let me set this out in the context of Genesis and then suggest an order for our oneness with God and others. That way, we'll see once more who we are and where we're meant to travel. The following chapter will help us do some analysis as to why we're missing out on oneness with God, why our travels are troubled.

Genesis

Did you ever pause when you read the words, "It is not good that the man should be alone" (Gen. 2:18)? God had already proclaimed creation "very good" (Gen. 1:31). So why was this "not good"? Did God forget to edit his rough draft of creation?

"Not good" here doesn't mean "bad." It means "unfinished." God had created a home for his creatures. Part of Adam's home was the garden and the animals. But a home is more than this. As creation is ultimately personal—spoken into being by the three-personed God—the hallmark of creation would be persons, *plural*. Adam would find his home in another. God takes something from inside Adam, his rib, to make something outside of him—his home, another person. Vern Poythress notes that the Hebrew word used here for the making of Eve is *banah*, a word often translated as "build," and this wasn't the common word used elsewhere for "make."[61] I like to think of it in terms of home building. "God made the woman in a manner analogous to a man building a house."[62] God built another *person* to be part of Adam's home.

This corresponds beautifully with the mysterious truth that each *person* of the Godhead is a home for the others. Each dwells in the others. If this is true, then Adam is not complete as an image-bearing creature until Eve is made. Adam was made for personal communion, for fellowship. As the moon was made to glow and the sun was made to shine, we were made for others. We were made for fellowship. We were made for oneness.

An Order for Oneness

But this doesn't mean that everyone was made for marriage. It means everyone was made for *fellowship*. Marriage is a special gift of fellowship, not a prerequisite for it.

Yet before we get too far, we need to note an order for oneness. It's critical to do this or else we'll get lost in the temporary and forget the eternal. Many people in the world only chase after oneness with another human being. They are all looking for love from another creature. As beautiful as that is, it wasn't our primary destiny. We were made *first* for oneness with God and *second* for oneness with others. That has to be the order. Otherwise we fall apart.

Let me get at it this way. Without a right relationship with God, there will necessarily be a rift in your relationships with others. The God who is three persons made you to be in intimate, loving fellowship with himself. Because God is the source of all relationships, when we're not right with him, all of our other relationships are off kelter, tilted like a table with a stone under one foot. To understand what it means to relate to others in loving-kindness, we need to be at one with the *God* of loving-kindness. This is what J. Gresham Machen meant when he said, "The relation to God is the all-important thing. It is not a mere means to an end.

Everything else is secondary to it."[63] He also says, "It is true that this world presents pressing problems, but you can never solve even those problems aright unless you first face the question of your relation to God."[64] Why would he say these things? Because our relationship with God affects everything else, including our relationships with others. Oneness with the relational God is the stone cast in the lake of the soul. The source of the ripples matters most. Our relationship with that source, with God, affects the rest of our relationships. That's why oneness with God must be primary.

This book will focus on our oneness with God: how it's achieved, maintained, and completed. But that will situate us to see what our oneness with others should look like. Oneness has an order: God first, then people. If you want to sound smart, you can say, "Anthropology follows theology." If you want to sound even smarter, find a way to say that in Latin. For the rest of us, it's enough to know that God comes first and people come second.

As an aside, if you're having trouble in particular relationships with someone, that *may* be because there's a problem or lack of development in your relationship with God. The two can't be pulled apart. If you're one with God, then you know what selfless love looks like. And if you're constantly communing with God in prayer and Scripture reading, he will be faithful in showing you how to display that selfless love to others. The details can get complex, but that's the basic truth.

Let me give you one example before we end the chapter. It can be easy for me to treat marriage as transactional sometimes. I imagine that's true for many people. Somewhere along the way, our hearts give in to the lie that marriage is basically a kinder form of *quid pro quo*. "You do this for me, and I'll do that for you." But that's a terrible way to view marriage, and we know it. Why? Because it's ultimately selfish. It's all about what *I* can get from someone else. But "love is patient and kind; love does not envy or boast; it is not arrogant or rude. It does not insist on its own way" (1 Cor. 13:4–5). Did you catch that last part? I can't get in the habit of insisting on my own way if I want to truly love my wife. Why? Because that's not how God loves, and God *is* love (1 John 4:8).

How exactly does God love? Just look at God's greatest act of love. "Greater love has no one than this, that someone lay down his life for his friends" (John 15:13). Love is self-giving, self-sacrifice. Love is wanting the best for someone else regardless of whether that involves you or gets you something.

Something should be coming into focus now: what we think about God affects how we engage with people. Our relationship with God, our oneness with him, affects our relationships with others. That's because oneness with God is primary; he's designed us that way, to relate to him first and others second. We can't expect to love others well without loving God first. I can't expect to love my wife well without first loving God well.

Being made for oneness means that all of our human relationships are linked to our divine relationship. Oneness has an order. We have to focus on our oneness with God if we want our oneness with others, our human relationships, to improve, to blossom like the rosebuds they are.

But there are many obstacles to our oneness with God, aren't there? That may even be why you're reading this book. It's certainly why I'm writing it!

We now have a knowledge of who God is and who we are, and we have the holy, perfect prayer of God himself for our oneness. If we have all of that, then why does oneness with God seem like a hazy dream more than a pulsing reality? Why is there an absence of oneness in our lives? We need to take a long look at that before we can connect where we are to where we should be. We'll do the latter by focusing on the path of oneness: our Spirit-wrought union with Christ.

Reflection Questions and Prayer

1. In what ways do you think our oneness with God differs from our oneness with other creatures?

2. What are some ways our human relationships can reflect problems in our relationship with God?

3. What does it look like practically to focus on oneness with God first? In other words, how does loving God with all our hearts differ from loving others as ourselves?

Prayer
Father, Son, and Spirit,
You made us for yourself.

You called us into holy relationship.
We're made to be one with you.
And out of that oneness
Flow our relationships with others.
Help us to keep you first,
To wake up speaking and listening to you,
To lie down speaking and listening to you.
Spirit, help us to engage with you as our first love.
Mend our broken soul
So that we might be a self-giving blessing
In all of our other relationships.

Reader Resource: Oneness with God and Oneness with Others

This chapter has argued that our oneness with God shapes and colors our oneness with other creatures. Difficulties in our relationship with God spill into difficulties in our human relationships. Below are some possible connections between our relational problems with God and our relational problems with people. What other connections would you add?

- **Selfishness.** When we only chase after God because we want something from him, that easily leads to the habit of chasing after others so that we can get what we want, not so that we can give what we have. It's impossible to be purely selfless with other people if we're selfish towards God. If our human relationships appear to be transactional—we're only a part of them so we can get something—it may very well stem from a transactional approach to our relationship with God. It helps to ask in prayer what we can *give* to God, instead of only asking him for what we need. There's nothing wrong with the latter, but it shouldn't be the only element of our prayers. Seek to give.

- **Apathy.** Some people find a relationship with God irrelevant and boring. They're convinced that there are more exciting things to sprint after in the world—money, possessions, sex, drug-induced sensations, etc. This leads to apathy towards God, an absence of care or interest. But this relational problem with God can contaminate our human relationships, too. We may only form human relationships based on the thrills or sensations they bring. When those thrills and sensations are absent, we stop caring about the relationship. Even the deepest of our relationships can turn into things we shrug at. If we're struggling with this, we need to seek out avenues for exploring the wildness and vigor of God. The all-powerful and ever-creative Father, Son, and Spirit are *anything* but boring. There's no problem with God, with his beauty and brilliance; the problem lives in our own heart. We're blind to God's immanence, his closeness to us in the everyday moments. As the Spirit helps us to see God all around us, we begin to understand that God is always relevant; he's always active in revealing himself to us. Learning to see God in the ordinary will affect the care we have for the human relationships he's blessed us with. For examples, see Tish Harrison Warren's *Liturgy of the Ordinary* and my *Finding God in the Ordinary*. Both books explore the presence of God in the everyday moments of life. This can help burn away the apathy we feel towards God and others.

- **Skepticism.** If we are constantly doubting God, we'll be constantly doubting others. Skepticism is often seen as a virtue in the West, something that keeps us from being deceived by the wild claims of religion. But skepticism builds walls. It isolates us. If we're skeptical of God, we're likely skeptical of others, always assuming they're out to get something for themselves, hiding their ulterior motives. While sin certainly makes the latter a reality, there is also the God-spoken truth that love is real and earnest. Love calls for trust, and trust isn't always rewarded with shame, as the skeptic fears. Trust may make us vulnerable, but rewards us with relationship, which is the very thing we were made for.

Chapter Seven

The Absence of Oneness

In one sense, this chapter was the easiest for me to write. I debated over whether to have this earlier in the book or later. But in the end, I decided that we have to know what oneness is and how God himself prayers for it (John 17) before we identify the ways in which we struggle to experience it. This chapter is about the struggle.

Being candid is always best, so I'll start with this: I'm an expert . . . at the absence of oneness. I have years of experience, years of grasping for it, years of it being on the horizon but not in my hands. Maybe you feel the same way.

There's a long list of things that get in the way of our oneness with God. This chapter is meant to be a survey and self-evaluation. I'll start with the theological causes and then move to the practical ones. Examine your own heart to see which ones are most prevalent for you, or if you might add other causes.

Theological Causes

Theologically speaking, oneness is only ever possible when the door of trust is kept open. You can't be one with someone you don't trust. And in the story of Scripture, distrust—the closing of the door between God and man—is what broke oneness in the first place.

Let's go back to Genesis again. At the dawn of time, we have a relationship. There is God the giver—Father, Son, and Spirit. And there is Adam and Eve, his reflectors. The setting is a garden, bursting with color and teeming with life.

Use your imagination. The air is heavy and sweet, filled with cedar wood and maple; the grass soft as silk; bird songs filling all the spaces among the canopies, like piano notes finding their homes amidst the silence. Pears, pomegranates, and figs so ripe and full that their branches hung low, offering the generosity of God in round, skinned packages of green and red. The rabbits and squirrels dancing through thickets, alert to the joy of abundance. And the sky—each day a song of light, running red to blue and then golden-orange, clouds sailing through like ships made by angel hands. This is the wild wonder of God's good earth. And into this wonder God whispered his shepherding words. "Eat from every tree but one." That's a call to trust in the beautiful, bountiful, generous God of creation. Trust—that was in focus for the first relationship, and for every relationship since. Trust.

This is always what God's words do. They set trust before us like a well-cushioned chair. "Sit," he says. "Sit and stay awhile. I'll take care of your needs. Just rest on the frame. Put all your weight in it. Nothing will whine or crack. You'll be alright."

We know that Adam and Eve wouldn't sit in the chair with all their weight. They believed a lie about God instead. And the lie spread. It spread to their progeny—a blood borne disease. It spread to you. It spread to me—the disease of distrust.

Distrust is the first and deepest cause for the breaking of oneness. Look at what happened as a result. Before the fall, Adam and Eve used to walk with God on well trodden paths through the garden. But after their distrust led to disobedience, they fled. They hid themselves. Do you see the visual depiction of how oneness breaks? There is distance now. There is hiding. There is shame. There is fear. That's what distrust does. Distrust takes the perfect circle of oneness and divides it, adding space between the persons.

Don't you ever feel like that, like there's this space between you and God? Rainer Maria Rilke had a few lines in one of his poems that always struck me.[65] In a sacred conversation with God, he writes,

> As it happens, the wall between us
> is very thin. Why couldn't a cry
> from one of us
> break it down? It would crumble
> easily,

it would barely make a sound.

Sometimes it feels like a thin wall stands between us and God. Other times it feels like the Atlantic runs between us, like we're continents apart. It seems hard for us to even notice him.

Distrust is most often a quiet disease. It creeps through the caverns of our thought, whispering "no" where "yes" should be, pushing our heads down so that we can't see God, chanting about how past failures must govern future freedom. And distrust is the devil's favorite melody. He's always humming it to us. And as long as we follow along with it, oneness with God is threatened.

We need trust to have loving, intimate fellowship with anyone. And with the invisible God who speaks, we need trust in his words. We need to sit in the worded frame he gives us in Scripture. Look at what Jesus says. "If anyone loves me, he will keep my words, and my Father will love him, and we will come to him and make our home with him" (John 14:23). Love is bound to keeping God's words. *Oneness* is bound to keeping God's words. Without fully trusting what God says—about who we are, about what we need, about how we approach suffering, about how we're being daily shaped to his image, about what we hope for—we can't be fully one with him.

Now, let me pause here to make a very important theological distinction. We'll talk soon about union with Christ as the path to oneness, but there is a very real sense in which your oneness with God goes well beyond your feelings. If you believe in Christ and have received the Spirit, you *are* one with God. Nothing and no one can take that away—not even the devil himself. So, when I say that we "can't be one with God" when distrust is present, I'm not talking about the deeper theological truth of our salvation. Our salvation is an objective fact, eternally set. Instead, I'm talking about our day to day *experience* with God. Even though we're joined to the Father in Christ and by the Spirit, we also haven't fully become who we will be (1 John 3:2). Or, perhaps better, we haven't fully realized who we *already* are in Christ. Paul talks about knowing one day in full, as he is fully known (1 Cor. 13:12). He's talking about the *experience* of oneness with God, not the objective truth of that oneness (salvation in Christ through faith).

The theological truth of our salvation and union with God is like a magnet for our souls. It's pulling us forward to the end. Nothing can stop that force. At the same time, we're not there yet. And you know that, don't you? You can feel it. Your experience of oneness hasn't caught up with the truth of your oneness. It's an already-but-not-yet reality. This parallels what John Owen wrote about our communion with God being *both* complete and incomplete.

Keep this in mind throughout the book. We're not working towards oneness as if we could earn it, as if we could somehow complete the unfinished jigsaw puzzle of our own salvation. But we *are* working out our salvation with fear and trembling (Phil. 2:12). We are striving in the Spirit to have the truth of our oneness match our daily experience. That's what faith is about: aligning our lives with the truth of God, recognizing along the way that

God is the one doing the aligning by his Spirit. And that is one of the many reasons why we worship him.

Okay, back to the theological causes for the absence of oneness. Distrust is really the parent of the other theological causes. Again, look at Adam and Eve. Distrust leads to three other causes: *disobedience, fear,* and *shame.*

Disobedience

We overlook disobedience perhaps because it seems more like an action than a cause. But it's one of the most harmful causes of our brokenness. It was the repeated disobedience of the prodigal son that made him so distanced from his father (Luke 15:11–32). Distrust lays the tracks for the train of disobedience. When you don't trust what God says—about himself, about you, about the world you live in—you're in the perfect position to trust *yourself* or someone else. Trusting no one isn't an option. It's either God, self, or others. That's it. Those who say they don't trust anybody aren't telling the whole truth. What they mean is that they only trust themselves. Other people walk through life chasing the popular idols of the world: power, fame, money, sex, euphoria. They trust others. They trust that what everyone else is hunting is what they should hunt. And the last group trusts God, and as a result starts to resemble him in beautiful ways. It all goes back to one of my favorite sentences from G. K. Beale: "What you revere you resemble, either for ruin or restoration."[66]

Disobedience takes us away from oneness with God and puts us in relationship with something that can't satisfy us. Take alcoholism, for example. An alcoholic acts on the idea that the feeling of drunkenness is enough. It satisfies a longing for careless euphoria, even numbness, that tries to be a stand-in for oneness with God. But every hangover is a reminder of the lie. And yet when the reminder wears off, the lie looks ripe enough to eat again. The cycle continues. The distance widens. The disobedience has clicked down the tracks of distrust. The absence of oneness is a raw, open cut. Something on the inside screams for attention on the outside.

This is how disobedience works. Just as Adam and Eve fled from God (a futile thing, by the way) after their disobedience, so do we. We try to get as far from the idea of being in intimate relation with God as we can. Distrust lays the tracks. Disobedience takes us down them. And then comes *fear* and *shame*.

Fear

Now, there are two types of fear. There's *reverential fear*. That's a good kind of fear. It's the kind that recognizes God's greatness, power, and control. "The fear of the Lord is the beginning of wisdom" (Prov. 9:10). Adam and Eve would've had that before they fell. The God who gave their lungs breath and their world color was worthy of that kind of fear. The second type of fear is the one we usually think of. Let's call it *breaking fear*, since it's a type of fear that shatters us. When we're scared or terrified, when we're worried about consequences or punishment, that's breaking fear. That's the sort that John had in mind when he said, "There is no fear in love, for perfect love casts out fear" (1 John 4:18). When we're one with God, there's no fear of punishment or condemnation (Rom. 8:1). That's because, as we'll get to soon enough, when God looks at us, he sees the righteousness and beauty of Jesus. We're one with Christ by the Spirit, and so what belongs to Christ—perfect righteousness and beauty—belongs to us. Our darker selves have burned away. We're new creatures (2 Cor. 5:17) still growing into our heavenly clothes.

In light of that distinction, it's clear that Adam and Eve would have had breaking fear after they sinned. They had fear of condemnation and punishment. And if those terms sound off-putting to you or outdated (and they do for many new Christians), think of it this way. Adam and Eve kicked over the protective fence of God's words. They went where they shouldn't have gone. They did what they knew they shouldn't do. This is the prototypical example of children disobeying the good command not to put their fingers on a hot stove. In addition to the pain they felt in the action came a fear. "Oh no! I did it. And I can't take it back!"

Condemnation is the *knowledge* that something has gone wrong, and you're responsible. Punishment is the *consequence*. Adam and Eve *knew* they had a *consequence*. That's why they hid. This knowledge of a consequence (condemnation and punishment) is what broke their oneness with God and drove them into hiding. It's the same thing when a toddler breaks a flower vase. The light in his world goes dim for a moment. And that's enough for him to jump behind the couch and close his eyes.

We can't be one with God when breaking fear is present. And we all deal with this sometimes. It can show up as self-loathing, when we feel like a failure in the simplest ways. It can show up in disbelief, when we quietly confess that we couldn't possibly be worth saving. It can show up in the terror of judgment, when we assume that bad things happening to us are a result of some pattern of sin. No matter how it manifests, breaking fear builds an invisible wall between us and God. Even if we're sitting right next to him on the other side, there's this thing that keeps us from feeling truly close to him. There's a barrier. And sometimes it's there so long we accept it as normal, passing it off as an aloofness that must be related to God's greatness.

Let me tell you something: God's greatness has *never* kept him from us. It's never kept us from being *his people*. Even in the presence of sin—the very first sin—God comes close and speaks. In fact, oneness with God is always about *him* coming to *us*, not the other way around. We worship a prodigal God, a God who spends all his love on us, not when we're worthy of it, but precisely when we're unworthy of it (Rom. 5:8), when we're raging against him, when we're kicking his words in the dirt and spitting on his Son. *He* comes to *us*. In fact, as Dane Ortlund has shown, our very fallenness is what draws out God's heart. "It is the very fallenness which he came to undo that is most irresistibly attractive to him. This is deeper than saying Jesus is loving or merciful or gracious. The cumulative testimony of the four Gospels is that when Jesus

Christ sees the fallenness of the world all about him, his deepest impulse, his most natural instinct, is to move toward that sin and suffering, not away from it."[67] Is that not wild? As the loving Father, as the sent Son, as the companioning Spirit, God is drawn to *us*, not just *despite* our sin but *because of* it. He sweeps our breaking fears aside as if they were bread crumbs on his ancient table, and he stares at us in love so strong that we're reborn in him, new children, progeny of God-given faith.

Shame

Distrust, disobedience, fear, and then *shame*. Adam and Eve were embarrassed. But did you ever think about why? It says in Genesis, "I was afraid, because I was naked" (Gen. 3:10). But then God says, "Who told you that you were naked?" (Gen. 3:11). Adam and Eve were naked *before* they distrusted and disobeyed. And they were naked *after* that, too. The nakedness wasn't the thing that changed. What changed? Their knowledge of it, their perception of it.

Think about this with me. When Adam and Eve "knew" about their nakedness, that doesn't mean that they *became* naked in God's presence; it means that they changed the way they saw themselves. Nakedness had never been an issue before. They were who they were before God without a thought. Nothing was between God and his people, not even clothing. There were no secrets, nothing "private" as opposed to "public." All was public between them. There was pure, interpersonal sharing among them. Shame entered only when there became something to hide, something to be kept private, something to cover.

Shame says, "Don't look. I don't want you to see this." It closes the door on oneness. It puts a covering over us. God sees right through it, of course. But that doesn't keep us from trying to cover up. We just don't want to be seen.

Some theologians talk about the first clothing of animal skins as a blessing (3:21). It wasn't a blessing, really. It was an accommodation of their shame. The clothing was God's way of saying, "Okay. You want to pretend that I don't see you? You want to pretend that you can keep things private from me? Go ahead. Play your game. It will cost life to play it. But you'll always be naked to me."

Just think of the irony. Adam and Eve already had skin—beautiful, adequate, God-made skin. Clothing was just another skin, an attempt to conceal what God could see anyway. Adam and Eve—like you and me—were trying to remake themselves in their own image; they were trying to cover what *they* thought needed covering, not what *God* thought needed covering. Clothing was their attempt to live in a world where oneness with God was broken. It was ultimately futile, as all sin is. But they did it anyway. They were embarrassed by how God had made them—to be fully seen and fully known. They were convinced they could do better, that they *had* to do better. Oneness with God was now always going to have a barrier before it, represented by their clothing.

I'm not advocating for nudist colonies, by the way. I'm just pointing out the theological and spiritual origin for covering ourselves. Nakedness is only a problem when we believe two things:

(1) that we have something that should be hidden and (2) that we think we can actually hide it. Both of those things happened once sin entered the picture. The tragedy of it all is that neither of those things has to be true.

There's nothing we should hide from God, and we're not able to hide anything anyway. That's why shame must be overcome by oneness. That's why Jesus took shame on his shoulders and crucified it with his naked body. Shame died with Jesus. And it didn't rise again. Jesus wore garments after his resurrection for *our* sake, not his. He had nothing to hide. We still think that we have things to hide and that we can actually hide them. That's shame.

Practical Causes

Distrust, disobedience, fear, and shame are what I've called the theological causes for the breaking of oneness. But there are several practical causes related to them that crop up in our daily lives. Let's look at these before we end the chapter and then walk steadily on the path to oneness with God in Christ.

Hurry

We live in a bustling world. Each of us stands amidst the noise and movement like a pigeon on a city street, cooing about the weather and the food scraps we've found. So much is going on around us, and we're more aware of it than we've ever been before.

What does this lead to? Frantic pigeons, snapping our heads in every direction. Because we're aware of too much, we're trying to do too much. Trying to do too much leads to our doing too many things with inadequate attention. In trying to do more too quickly, we do less. This is hurry.

Hurry is a result of saying "yes" to everything. But we don't see this until it's too late. John Mark Comer writes, "Every yes is a thousand nos. Every activity we give our time to is a thousand other activities we *can't* give our time to."[68] We ignore this. We act instead as if every yes is a *yes—and*. "Can I do social media?" Yes—*and* pour a good chunk of time into reading my Bible." "Can I keep my head in a Netflix series for a bit? Yes—*and* still find a way to concentrate in prayer." *Yes—ands* are corrosive to spiritual oneness. Why? As Mary Oliver put it, "Attention is the beginning of devotion."[69] Our attention is limited because *we* are limited. The more we give away, the less we have. And oneness with God requires our attention, especially in Scripture reading and prayer. But aren't these the first things to go when we feel busy? Why is it that "the things that are truly life-giving for your soul are the first to go rather than your first *go to*?"[70] Maybe it's because we're not fully convinced that these things *are* life-giving. Maybe, like Adam and Eve, we doubt that what God says about keeping his words and being one with him (John 14:23) is really true.

That is a huge problem. Let me put this more starkly, as Comer did. "Hurry is a form of violence on the soul."[71] Think about that: violence on the soul. Hurry isn't just a lifestyle decision; it's a corrosive disease. It eats away at your attention, which is one of the most precious gifts you can give to God. In fact, without regularly giving that gift, your oneness with him will suffer. Oneness with God is a relationship, and relationships require time and attention. Time and attention are the oxygen of love; without them, relationships are bound to wither.

Do you struggle with hurry? I certainly do. I have to practice saying no to more things so that I can say yes to my relationship with the Lord.

Comer developed a little checklist of symptoms for what he called "hurry sickness."[72] If you put a check mark next to a few of these, then hurry needs to be addressed with more nos if you want deeper oneness with God.

- Irritability
- Hypersensitivity
- Restlessness
- Workaholism (or just non-stop activity)
- Emotional numbness
- Out-of-order priorities
- Lack of care for your body
- Escapist behaviors
- Slippage of spiritual disciplines

- Isolation

Hurry is actually related to all of the theological causes for our lack of oneness. It's related to distrust, for example, because our hurry often suggests that we trust our own abilities more than God's truth. Think about it. Do you and I *really* live as if the words of God are our primary nutrition (Deut. 8:3; Matt. 4; John 4:34)? Or do we trust that going after a list of other things is really going to be more fulfilling? I'm as guilty as everyone else. I struggle each day in little ways to trust that God really knows what's best for my soul: oneness with him.

Distraction

Distraction is a fractured window; it's hard to see anything through it with detail. The division of the whole means less depth, less attention, less care. You can see how that would be a problem for oneness with God.

And if hurry is, as Comer put it, a form of violence on the soul, then distraction is the open wound that refuses to heal. It keeps hurting us, but in a measure small enough to keep our focus elsewhere—our broken, divided focus. Distraction hurts us just enough to keep us trapped, to cage our souls so that movement and growth become impossible. Don't you and I want to get out of the cage?

Some weeks ago, we had a groundhog living under our shed. We called someone out to trap it humanely. He set up cages around the groundhog's entrance, and we caught him the next day. But we left the traps there for another day just to make sure there weren't others. The following morning I found a rabbit inside one of the cages.

I had been taught how to open the cage in case something like this happened, so I went out to set it free. When I got closer, my heart sank. I love animals and hate to see them in pain. The rabbit was flooded with fear that poured out of his big, black eyes. As I got closer, he kept darting back and forth frantically, searching for an exit in the presence of a lumbering giant. Its nose was bleeding from trying to push open the locked door. I opened the door as quickly as I could, and the rabbit shot through the grass like a bullet, jumping into the open expanse of freedom.

You and I are like that rabbit. Distraction is our cage. Only we seem less frantic about breaking free. In fact, we live as if there were no cage. But there is.

A 2019 study found that the average American checks his phone once every ten minutes.[73] That's 96 times a day. That was a 20% increase from a similar survey two years before. So, it's likely gotten worse. One person claimed it's up to 262 checks a day in 2021.[74] That's once every five minutes or so. Let's work with that figure for now.

Once every five minutes, Americans stop whatever they're doing to check their phone, to look into a virtual window that offers access to other worlds. Once every five minutes, we're leaving where we are to go somewhere we cannot be. That's unprecedented in human history. *Unprecedented.* And unprecedented things usually make us blind to their effects.

How is this distraction affecting our oneness? For starters, how many times do you check in with God each day? Once in the morning, an occasional thought throughout the day, maybe a prayer if things are hard and loved ones are hurting, and then that ritualized before-dinner prayer. So, maybe five times a day, give or take. Five vs. 262. The bigger number eats the smaller number.

How can we possibly expect to grow in our oneness with God if we give it so little attention, if we speak to God so infrequently, if we listen to his voice in Scripture so fleetingly? We can't. Let me say it again. *We can't.* Distraction does not allow devotion. You choose one or the other. Actually, you *keep* choosing one or the other all throughout the day.

This book won't focus on creating a strategy for you to defeat distraction. That's a project in itself. But it will show you the path to oneness in the next chapter and offer some tools to that end. You and I will need to choose daily—even hourly—if we're going to walk that path.

Distraction, deep down, is also linked to distrust. It says, "This thing will be better and more entertaining than what God offers." That doesn't seem like distrust, but it is. Our hearts go where we trust. Our time goes to our treasures. Do we trust that oneness with God is the most fulfilling thing in the universe? If we do, we will act on that trust. If we don't, we'll go elsewhere.

Lesser Loves

Not all lights are created equal. Some are dim and sapped of gold. Others glow and draw a crowd. Others are steady and silent, lighting just enough of their surroundings to provide a humble home. But not every humble home is a good home. Not every light demands devotion. And there is only one that deserves it. We might call it the Father light (James 1:17).

Loves are like lights, aren't they? They enter the wide pupils of the soul. They attract. They ask for entrance, and we give it to them. The trouble is that oneness with God requires devotion to the Father light, the greatest light, the North Star of spirits. When we follow other lights, oneness fades. That's because of how we've been made. We're wicks crafted for one flame, wound and ready for his passion, the spark of his self-giving love, to bury itself in our dry fibers and ignite us.

But receiving that light takes patience, silence, and faith. It's a matter not just of wanting, but of *waiting*. And as we wait, other lights drift before us, other loves beckoning in the black.

Anything you like can be a light: a feeling, an activity, a person. The trouble isn't the expanse of lights. It's our reordering of the spiritual solar system to make lesser lights the center of the universe, to take good things and make them god things. Whenever we do this—and we're tempted every day—oneness with God wanes. Remember what we saw in the previous chapter: oneness with God needs to take precedence over oneness with others, and over our passion for other things.

Lies

The last impediment to our oneness with God is as common as it is ancient: *lies*. Many lies keep us from uniting with the God who is truth (John 14:6). But I'll focus on the greatest one: the lie that the Father, Son, and Spirit are not real, are not present, and thus can't be communed with. Few Christians would admit to believing this lie, but many of us live as if it were true. Just ask yourself how often you talk to God and whether you *really* believe that someone is listening. We act as if we're in a room by ourselves. Just because we speak doesn't mean we believe we're communicating. Speech must be accompanied by belief.

Living as if God were not present is an ancient problem. Could Eve had taken fruit from the forbidden tree if she truly believed that God was present, that he was with her? God's invisibility is a cloak for his omnipresence. And that cloak has always served as a test of our belief. Will we truly live as if God was present, as if he was always in the room, beneath us, behind us, and before us?

The lie that God is not present may very well be the most potent lie that's ever existed. And it's plain how this lie would block our oneness with God. You can't be one with someone you're not sure is here.

Again, this lie is so powerful, in part because we don't want to admit that we believe it. But honesty is the door to healing. If we don't start by opening that door, we'll never address the problem.

Summary

Now, we've covered a lot in this chapter, so let's put it all together. Below are the reasons we covered for the absence of our oneness with God. Keep in mind the earlier distinction that our union with Christ, the subject of the next chapter, establishes our union with God, our oneness with him. In that sense, we are already one with God once we're joined to Christ by the Spirit. But our oneness isn't yet consummated. That's what John Owen meant when he said our communion with God was currently "initial and incomplete." Our oneness with God is being assaulted all the time. It's in the latter sense that oneness can seem absent. I say this not simply because it's true but because it's an encouragement. You don't have to go out and get oneness; you already have it in seed form. Nothing can kill the seed, but you and I need to work with the Spirit to cultivate it.

- Distrust
- Disobedience
- Fear
- Shame
- Hurry
- Distraction

- Lesser loves

- Lies

Now that we've seen what oneness is, where it's rooted (in the triune God), how Jesus himself prayed for it, and what keeps us from it, we're ready to walk the path of oneness, fully aware of the threats. No one should walk blindly into battle.

Reflection Questions and Prayer

1. Where can you identify distrust in your relationship with God?

2. Which of the theological causes for our lack of oneness with God do you most struggle with?

3. Which of the practical causes do you most struggle with? Would you add any others?

Prayer
So much.
So much gets in the way, Lord.
You made us to be one with you.
And we fell away.
We *keep* falling away.
We keep getting interrupted.

Our distrust paralyzes us.
Our hurry dazes us.
We chase after lesser loves.
God, help us.
Spirit, open our hearts
To the brilliance of your presence.
Guide our feet towards you
In all of the little moments.
Keep us vigilant of threats and idols
That steal our attention.
Help us to *see*
With the eyes of faith
And to act on that vision.

Chapter Eight

THE PATH TO ONENESS

Union with Christ

You and I know several things at this point. We know that we yearn for oneness with God. We know that we were made for it. We know why we were made for it: we're made in God's image, and God is a union of three persons in one essence. We're made for relationship, both with him and with each other. We also know that this oneness is so important that the Son of God prays for it. He prays that we would be one with him in order to show the world that God sent him. It's only when we're in communion with God, when we're one with him, that our human relationships can reach their full potential. We also know that we often lack this oneness, or at least we don't feel it. And even though faith goes beyond feelings, there's something to be said for experiencing a deeper union with God. If John Owen is right, that our communion with God is currently initiated but incomplete, then we should be looking for progress towards completeness, shouldn't we? Amidst the obstacles to deeper union with God, we need a path that will take us further up and further in. We need a mountain climber's path, as Paul had. We need Christ.

And now we come to it: the ancient path to oneness with God. This is *your* path; this is *my* path. We need to know it better than we know our own faces. We need to be able to walk it with our eyes closed. So, take your time with this chapter. This is the way to oneness with God—the greatest thing imaginable.

Let's first describe what it is. Then we can make a distinction. And we'll spend the rest of the chapter noting how we walk on this path in everyday life. In the remaining chapters, we'll talk about oneness in private, oneness in public, and the destiny of oneness. My hope is to give you a road map for your spiritual life so that you can monitor your own steps on the path and return to the center when you drift to the right or left.

What Is Union with Christ?

The phrase "union with Christ" sounds so abstract, doesn't it? We tend to push abstractions to the periphery and focus on particulars. Let me try to particularize this as best I can.

Do some digging. What does it mean to be one with another person? We've already talked about oneness in the context of who God is, who we are, and what Jesus prayed for. So, you should have some idea. In Jesus's prayer, and in our earlier discussions about oneness, we noted that oneness is about *love* and *fellow-*

ship. But what does that really mean when we're talking about Jesus? How do we experience love and fellowship with a two-thousand-year-old resurrected Nazarene? I believe the answer lies in two words: *heart* and *will*.

Our *heart* is the spring of our desire and devotion. What trickles from its hidden caverns is what we most long for. Jesus said, "Where your treasure is, there will your heart be also" (Luke 12:34). Treasure can be beautiful or beastly. It can glimmer with the glory of eternity, or it can pull the light from our eyes and replace it with darkness (Mark 7:20–23). The heart builds its home around our treasure. It beats in step with our love, our yearning.

Our *will* is the riverbed for heart water. It takes our longing and carries it to thought, speech, and action. Will without heart is madness; heart without will is a cesspool. We need both. We need both the longing and the leading, the passion and the practice, the depth and the diligence.

You and I have this already, whether or not we know it. Right now, at this very moment, you have a longing that is being channeled into thought, speech, and action. Or perhaps several longings. Do you know what they are? Pause and ponder. What do you treasure right now? Where has your will brought you today?

Now, here's the next phase in our digging. What is the heart and will of Christ? Being one with him will mean *sharing* his heart and will. If you don't know what they are, how could you possibly be one with him?

These elements, heart and will, are essential to identity. If someone asked you who Jesus is and what he's like, what would you say?

What is his heart and will? We have to know the answer to those questions.

In Dane Ortlund's beautiful book *Gentle and Lowly*, he focuses on the heart of Jesus.[75] Jesus, in fact, tells us what his heart is; he sets it in the open air before us, and it's something we wouldn't expect.

Remember here that we're talking about the depths of God, his heart. And "the heart, in biblical terms, is not part of who we are but the center of who we are. Our heart is what defines and directs us."[76] Are you ready? Here is the heart of Christ, the Son of light and life, very God of very God: "I am gentle and lowly in heart" (Matt. 11:29).

Gentle . . . "not harsh, reactionary, easily exasperated. He is the most understanding person in the universe. The posture most natural to him is not a pointed finger but open arms."[77]

Lowly . . . He's come right down to our level. We can approach him. In fact, "no one in human history has ever been more approachable than Jesus Christ."[78]

According to Jesus Christ himself, this is his heart. "Open. Welcoming. Accommodating. Understanding. Willing."[79] The heart of Christ moves towards others. He moves towards the closed, the unwelcome, the stubborn, the ignorant, the unwilling. The heart of Christ gravitates towards its opposite, and then it makes that opposite like him.

Christ didn't come to friends in the cold and turning earth. He came to enemies. And yet, "while we were still sinners, Christ died for us" (Rom. 5:8). Christ's heart for us is what made our hearts for him.

How is this possible? It's possible because God is love (1 John 4:8), and love "bears all things, believes all things, hopes all things, endures all things" (1 Cor. 13:7). The heart of Christ, the heart of God, bore us, believed us, hoped us, and endured us into himself. And the heart of Christ did that because love is essentially self-giving.

God in Christ held nothing back. He gave all of himself, and he did that because all of him was love. And if love is self-giving, then love must also be open, welcoming, accommodating, understanding, and willing. Love must be gentle and lowly. That is the heart of Christ.

And his will? He tells us in a food metaphor that I've always smiled at. What does Jesus need even more than bodily sustenance? More than dried fish and hard bread? "My food is to do the will of him who sent me and to finish his work" (John 4:34). Jesus's will is to do the will of his Father. Don't you love that? How could it be otherwise if Jesus and the Father are one? They share the same will along with the Spirit. Three persons, one will.

But what is that will? What is the monumental action that bursts from the heart of God? It was an action of *love*. That is who God is. "For God so loved the world, that he gave his only Son" (John 3:16). Do you see it, the divine poetry of heart and will? Love leads to giving of self!

The heart and will of God for men

Came with bones and skin and blood.
He laid his body down and then
Drew souls up from the mud.

What does all this mean? It means that *the heart and will of Christ is gentle, lowly, and self-giving*. If you are one with Christ, by the Spirit of love, then *you* will be gentle and lowly and self-giving. And the more gentleness, lowliness, and self-giving soak into your soul, the closer to God you will be.

What Union Involves

Now, let's revisit that distinction that I mentioned in a previous chapter, the already-but-not-yet dimension of communion with God. We can also use the terms *union* and *communion*. Union isn't something you work on. It's something God does. And we're united to Christ by the Spirit. This is so richly personal. You and I are joined to the *person* of Christ by the *person* of the Spirit. Person to person by person.

This union goes beyond words, but it reaches into the mystery of oneness that Christ speaks of in John 17. Despite what we've already said about union with Christ being an alignment of our heart and will with his, John Murray wants to push beyond this into a mystery indescribable:

> It is not simply the union of feeling, affection, understanding, mind, heart, will, and purpose. Here we

have a union which we are unable to define specifically. But it is a union of an intensely spiritual character consonant with the nature and work of the Holy Spirit so that in a real way surpassing our analysis Christ dwells in his people and his people dwell in him.[80]

Dwelling. A home in a person, and his home in us. That's union. We live here, in this union, right now. And we're never moving. The fact that this seems indescribable isn't too surprising. What would you say if someone were to ask you, "*What's* your home?" Not "where do you live?" or "what does your house look like?" but "*What's* your home?" *What* is it? Isn't that impossible to describe? Our minds start grasping at memories and feelings and comforts and a deep sense of rest, of belonging. If you ask me *what* my home is, my mouth will close. I won't know what to say. But I'll know my home more deeply than anything else. Scripture is telling us that *Christ* is our home, and we are his. That's union. It's already come, and it lives throughout eternity. I love the lines from Gerhardt Tersteegen's old hymn:

> He and I in one bright glory
> Endless bliss shall share:
> Mine, to be forever with him;
> His, that I am there.

Union means Christ is our home, and we are his. Forever. This is different from communion. And oneness with God involves both. Communion is closer to fellowship, as we noted. But you can't have communion if you don't have union. Paul writes, "God is faithful, by whom you were called into the fellowship of his Son, Jesus Christ our Lord" (1 Cor. 1:9). A. W. Pink writes,

> the word fellowship signifies such a co-partnership between persons that they have a joint-interest in one and the same enjoyment which is common between them. Now this fellowship or communion with Christ is entirely dependent upon our union with him, even as much as the branch's participation of the sap and juice is dependent upon its union and coalition with the stock of the tree. Take away union, and there can be neither communion nor communication.[81]

Communion stands upon union. And communion, as Pink notes, suggests we have "one and the same enjoyment." Can you guess what that is? Gentle and lowly self-giving—the heart and will of Christ.

What Does Union with Christ Look Like?

The Spirit unites us to Christ so that we can be more intimate with him, so that *his* heart and will become *our* heart and will. But this is still so hard to grasp, isn't it? What does union with Christ really look like? How can we understand it in a way that makes it easier to live out each day? What does it look and feel like to have union with Christ be our *path* to oneness, to loving fellowship with God?

We need to start by switching on our imagination. Would you do that with me? We're talking about being united with a two-thousand-year-old Nazarene, who is also the eternal Son of God. We can't approach this without turning on the lamp of imagination. We won't see anything without it. Why? Rankin Wilbourne reminds us that "Union with Christ is an enchanted reality. And we live in a disenchanted world."[82] *Enchanted.* The work of God in saving and redeeming souls steps outside the footpath of logic. It goes into the wild, where stories reign. And this is the greatest story of all time. You are in it. Right now. But to realize yourself in it, you have to light the wick of wonder, to let your imagination roam. "We must use our imagination if we want to fully inhabit and experience the Christian life. . . . believing the gospel means having your imagination taken captive and reshaped by a new story."[83]

A Story

Let me tell you a story. I'll tell it about myself. But you can do the same. Write it down. This will be a story *worth* saving, because it is a story *of* saving.

There once was a boy named Pierce Taylor Hibbs. He was born in a fishing town in Nova Scotia, Canada in the mid 1980s. His childhood was filled with the sound of swishing grass and wind in the trees. He saw the golden siding of his home, the broad bark of the sugar maple on the side of the yard, the blood-red leaves of autumn, and the heavy white blankets of long winters. The world was his canvas. He marked it everyday with his hands, with his feet, with his voice. All throughout the movement and the sound and the sweetness of maple syrup, there was a gap, something silent and deep inside him, a question mixed with longing. "Where am I going?" He never asked it out loud. He just kept it beneath him all day and all night.

But then one of those nights, he asked his father. His father told him that there was a man who cut a trail into the golden fields of eternity. If he believed in this man, then he would see the fields.

And so the boy decided. He would do this thing; he would . . . *believe*. What he didn't know is that as soon as he made that decision, his little life was planted. His soul was set in the soil. And something amazing began to happen in the silence and sound and movement of his little life: another person started to grow inside him. He was now a seed that contained a seed. Both were growing.

He didn't notice it for years. But then one day on a family vacation, as he walked through a local craft display off the coast of Massachusetts, he saw a yellow glass guitar, an ornament, strung with fishing line, dangling and spinning in the sun. The boy's father loved to play the guitar. And something inside him—this silent, second seed, this other person—prodded his hand into his pocket, where he found a ten-dollar bill. He took it out and bought the guitar for his father. As the craftsman handed him the brown paper bag, the boy realized the world was much greater than he thought. He was smaller than he realized, like a butterfly in an open field. So much was going on around him. So much had happened before him. His smallness was a gift.

And he understood then that someone else was growing inside him. His blood was not his own. Someone else—who *was* is?—was taking the reins of his life. Someone else was in charge of where he was going. Someone he couldn't see.

He asked his father about this. Did he, too, have another person living inside him? His father smiled and said, "Yes. Yes, I do." And the boy begged, "But who is he? What does he want? How can I speak with him?" The father handed him a black leather book and said, "He's in here. His *voice* is in here. And you can speak to him any time you like."

The boy took the book and stared at the cover. The black leather was as mysterious to him as his future. But he held it that night and whispered, "Hello."

Your Story

What's your story? Have you opened your imagination to this mystery of union with Christ?

Union with Christ goes beyond the realm of facts, with their clear landscapes and sky-scraping mountains. It goes through the mist, into the wild of love, where persons dwell. And Christ is an ancient person. Here's Wilbourne again: "God has called you into a new life, rooted in a history that predates you, anchored in the life, death, and resurrection of Jesus. . . . The lifeblood of another flows within you and gives you life. . . . You no longer belong only to yourself. Your identity now includes another; it is broadened from 'me' to 'us.'"[84]

Do you feel the mystery? This is the path to oneness with God. The path is a person. How do you walk it? With words.

The Centrality of Speech

In the next chapter, I want to sit at a table with this idea: The Word has died for you, now lives in you, and you need words to commune with him. You can't have a relationship with someone without words. Christ is the invisible someone living inside you, along with the Father and the Spirit. Do you exchange words with them?

I'm not talking about a tool for spiritual development. Words are much more than that. They are the currency of communion. And that is precisely what the Christian life is all about. The beating heart of faith flutters at the thought of communion with God because that's the very thing we're made for. Communion with God is The Great Gift. "Union with Christ is the doorway to communion with God. Christ, in uniting his life to ours, gives us access to the presence of God the Father (Eph. 2:18). And every other gift that God gives pales in comparison to this gift of God himself."[85]

The Great Gift is our greatest longing, the thing we yearn for most. It's the longing for union. Our hearts tilt up towards the light when we hear, "God has made a way for humanity to be joined to him by becoming one with us."[86] Don't bother trying to explain it. You can't explain how three divine persons can house themselves in a human. Perhaps because we can't explain it, we don't believe it. We close our mouths. We sit silent.

But the longer we sit silent, the more accustomed we grow to living as if God were mute, the further from him we'll feel. The path to oneness with God is paved with words. We have to listen and speak.

Christ is not, however, trying to whisper in your ear. His voice is etched into the pages for you in promises and prayers. John 17 isn't the only one. In fact, all of Scripture speaks of Christ. "The one spoken of on the pages is the same one who speaks through them. So you can come to the Bible expecting to hear from and commune with the one who stands at the center of it: Christ. Union with Christ is how the Bible becomes a burning bush out of which God speaks."[87]

I've set oneness as the answer to basic questions. Who are we? Where are we going? How will we get there? Let's draw these threads together now.

We are creatures made for communion, made for oneness with God. He is our destination, the one we're moving towards. And, paradoxically, we get there by being united to him in Christ, a union carried out by the Spirit. We unite with Christ by embracing his heart and will—gentle and lowly self-giving. But we also commune with God through words, since they are what birth and blanket all relationships. The path to oneness focuses on heart, will, and words.

Let me end with an example to bring all of this together, setting us up for the focus of the next chapter. Then we can talk about cultivating oneness with God in private so that the world will see that oneness in public. Remember, Jesus is clear in John 17 that our oneness with him is meant to be a witness to the watching world.

An Example of Communion

I opened my Bible to Acts and prayed a simple prayer: "God, please open my ears. Let me hear you speak to me. Let me hear your voice for this day." And then I read Acts 1:1–2:24. That was the voice of God to me this morning. As the clovers outside swayed in the gaze of dawn, as the sound machine in my daughter's room sent white noise down the hallway, as the coffee dripped into the pot and clouds seemed to grin against the light blue sky at their backs, God spoke.

He told me about Jesus rising and revealing himself. He told me about Jesus teaching on the kingdom of God and baptism in the Holy Spirit—repentance dipped in God. He told me about the pouring out of the Spirit, a holy fire that put words in the mouths of men. And he told me that Jesus's death and resurrection was part of the plan of our Father. And—my favorite part—he told me that it was not possible for death to hold down the Son of God. Life wins over death.

It's still quiet in the house, but I've been spoken to. The Christ to whom my soul is united clung to me as the Spirit began weaving words into my mind, the Father watching it all unfold perfectly, just as he planned it.

And now it's my turn to speak back, to stamp my feet on the path of union with Christ. I write exactly what I said. First, I rehearse the truth. Then I find myself in it.

> God . . . God, Christ rose from the dead. He came back. Jesus, you came back. And you spoke of a kingdom I know so little about. Show me where I am in your kingdom.

> Spirit, I see you poured out. And when men received you, they spoke. The many tongues of the world came together to speak about *one* thing: your mighty works. From diversity came unity. And the greatest, the mightiest work, was the death of death—the resurrection. Death could not hold you down. And this was all part of the plan, my Father. It's beyond my tired head this morning. I know the kids will be up soon. They will have no idea that you and I were speaking, that there were really four of us in the living room. What do you want me to focus on when they come out? . . . Yes, the resurrection, the death of death, the hope that dove into the black water of mortality and burst back out in light, for love. *A resurrection of light . . . for love*. Yes—that's it. Spirit,

you know how forgetful I am. Please keep bringing this to my remembrance. *A resurrection of light for love.* Help me to chant this when my patience wanes, when distraction grabs at me from every direction, when my heart strives for its own good. Replace my thoughts with this one. Let my speech today be colored by it. I am yours, and you are mine. Give your heart and will to me, my resurrected Lord.

After I finish speaking, there's no seismic shift. Everything looks and sounds and smells as it did before I spoke and before I heard the voice of God. But I *did* hear the voice of God. And I spoke back. This is the simple, faith-paved path to oneness with God. One conversation at a time, I learn more of him, and he reveals more to me. And now we have our conversation topic for today: a resurrection of light for love. I'll be muttering that phrase throughout the day.

Christ-Centered Interpretation

Maybe you noticed one missing component in all of this. How can I commune with *Christ* in every passage of Scripture I read? What if the passage I'm reading is some obscure text about sacrificial laws in Leviticus? Or a narrative of someone else's life? Or general principles on how to live wisely? A passage such as Acts 1:1–2:24 is clearly about Christ and his resurrection life, but how do I commune with Christ when I can't see him in the text?

The answer is easy but dense. Here's the easy part: *every passage in the Bible is about Christ*. Iain Duguid puts it plainly,

> The Old Testament is not primarily a book about ancient history or culture, though it contains many things that are historical and that describe ancient cultures. Centrally, the Old Testament is a book about Christ, and more specifically, about his sufferings and the glories that will follow—that is, it is a book about the promise of a coming Messiah through whose sufferings God will establish his glorious, eternal kingdom. . . . when we interpret the Old Testament correctly, without allegory or artificial manipulation but in accordance with Jesus's own teaching, the central message on every page is Christ. That does not mean that every verse taken by itself contains a hidden allusion to Christ, but that the central thrust of every passage leads us in some way to the central message of the gospel.[88]

This teaching comes from Jesus himself (Luke 24:25–27; 44–47), in addition to the Apostle Paul (Acts 26:22–23; 1 Pet. 1:10–11). All of Scripture, every passage, is about Christ. Put differently, "The Bible is Christ-centered. Covenants mediate God's presence to us, and at the heart of the covenants is Christ, who is the *one* mediator between God and men (1 Tim. 2:5)."[89] Christ is always at the center of a biblical passage.

The question is, how do we see this, since it isn't immediately apparent in Old Testament passages? Since many of the challenges lie with interpreting Old Testament passages in a Christ-centered way, let's focus there. How about a passage such as Leviticus 1:1–9?

> The LORD called Moses and spoke to him from the tent of meeting, saying, ² "Speak to the people of Israel and say to them, When any one of you brings an offering to the LORD, you shall bring your offering of livestock from the herd or from the flock. ³ "If his offering is a burnt offering from the herd, he shall offer a male without blemish. He shall bring it to the entrance of the tent of meeting, that he may be accepted before the LORD. ⁴ He shall lay his hand on the head of the burnt offering, and it shall be accepted for him to make atonement for him. ⁵ Then he shall kill the bull before the LORD, and Aaron's sons the priests shall bring the blood and throw the blood against the sides of the altar that is at the entrance of the tent of meeting. ⁶ Then he shall flay the burnt offering and cut it into pieces, ⁷ and the sons of Aaron the priest shall put fire on the altar and arrange wood on the fire. ⁸ And Aaron's sons the priests shall arrange the pieces, the head, and the fat, on the wood that is on the fire on the altar; ⁹ but its entrails and its legs he shall wash with water. And

the priest shall burn all of it on the altar, as a burnt offering, a food offering with a pleasing aroma to the LORD.

Where is Christ here? Vern Poythress offers three tools we can use to find him. Each of them relates to how the Old Testament deals with *time*.

> We have three main ways in which an Old Testament text can speak about time: (1) it can directly speak about the future; (2) it can speak about all times through a focus on general principles; and (3) it can speak about one specific time—but then this one specific time has relations to all the other times.[90]

Passages that speak about the future are always in some way speaking about the future fulfillment of the *promise* of God, the promise of "a coming Messiah through whose sufferings God will establish his glorious, eternal kingdom" (Duguid). Passages that speak about all times through a focus on general principles are in some way speaking about Christ, who is the fulfillment of all truth (John 14:6), wisdom (1 Cor. 1:24), righteousness (1 Cor. 1:30; 2 Cor. 5:21), and any other good principle or axiom you can imagine. Passages that speak about one specific time are organically rooted in a redemptive path that leads to Christ's person and work, often including *symbols* ("a concrete representation of divine truth," p. 241) and *types* (symbols that have a future fulfilment or realization).[91] Of course, some biblical passages speak of time in more than one sense, and so these categories could all apply to a single passage. In sum, we have passages of promise, passages of principle, and passages of particular history (involving symbols and types that point to Christ).

Let's apply these to the Leviticus passage. First, note that we already have more than one way of referencing time in this passage. The author is laying out general principles or rules for offering sacrifices (passages of principle). At the same time, these rules are presented to Israel at particular stage of their history (passages of particular history). There are also senses in which this passage is prophetic of Christ (passages of promise) through its symbols and types.[92]

Let's look at the recurring themes in the passage to get a sense of what the passage is about and how it's ultimately about Christ.

Offerings. The offerings discussed in this passage are meant to atone for sin (v. 4). This idea of atoning for sin via offering is strange to many modern readers. How does killing a bull help someone's sin situation? Doesn't that just make it worse, adding violence to moral failure? This isn't the place to get into a lengthy discussion of offerings and atonement, but think of it this way: all sin costs something. In fact, our rebellion against God is costly *to him*, not just to us. If sin costs something, then we might think of offerings as a means of payment. What has the highest value to God? What currency are we talking about here? It's not gold or jewels; it's *blood*. Blood is where life lives (Lev. 17:10–14). Blood is a sacred, spiritual currency. It's precious, and so it makes sense that the damages of sin could only be covered by this most sacred form of payment. And yet, we know that the payment is repeated, thousands, even millions of times. Why? Because sin had no one-for-all solution. That is, until Christ (Heb. 10:1–14). Christ was the costliest offering—*infinitely* costly, in fact. Nothing will ever *add* to the sacrifice of Christ, to the currency of *his* holy blood. It's fully sufficient. It's final.

In the light of Christ's fulfillment of the sacrificial system, we can say that the offerings in Leviticus 1:1–9 are *types*, pointing to a future fulfillment. As I read the passage, I think, "Christ, you are the most holy, most sufficient, most satisfying offering for your people. You were complete, beautiful, and perfect, 'without blemish.' Thank you for your all-sufficient offering, and thank you for showing me how your people were always reaching out their hands for *you*, even when they weren't aware of it." I'm reading Leviticus, but I'm communing with *Christ*.

Atonement. Atonement, we said, was the purpose of the offering in Leviticus 1:1–9. Atonement, though it can sound stuffy and traditional to today's readers, is deeply *relational*. It's about being one with God, having no barriers between us. We need atonement if we want *relationship*. The guidelines for satisfying atonement in this passage are ultimately about the all-atoning person of Christ, the purest offering. Christ is the one mediator between God and man (1 Tim. 2:5); he's the only one who can bring about perfect atonement for each of us. The temporary atonement in this Leviticus passage is, once again, a *type* (a forward-looking symbol) that directs our gaze to God's Son. I read about the Levites striving after priestly atonement, and I think, "Jesus, you are my high priest. You atoned for it *all*. Because of *you*, I have a relationship with God. More than that—I have *adoption* into his family!" Once more, I'm reading Leviticus, but I'm communing with *Christ*.

Blood. Blood is involved in the themes of offering and atonement, so I'll just touch on it briefly. It's another *type*, pointing forward to the only blood that can eternally atone. But what I find fascinating is that redemption happens inside and moves to the outside. Think about it. Blood houses life (Lev. 17:10–14), and the life of God is also *love* (1 John 4:8). That blood, running in tiny rivulets inside the body of Jesus Christ, is love-giving life. And love is what washes over a multitude of sin (1 Pet. 4:8). So, there's a sense in which *blood* washes over a multitude of sins. What lies on the inside comes to the open air to redeem the outside, to begin a new story that mends the torn tapestries of creation. Every time I read the word "blood" in the Bible, I think, "Christ, that river inside you that housed the very source of creation—you gave *that* for me. You gave your insides to heal my insides, so that the world outside might know that you've been sent. Thank you for your blood and the new story it's telling, even now." Again, I'm reading Leviticus, but I'm communing with *Christ*.

On the surface, Leviticus 1:1–9 is about guidelines for offering an animal sacrifice, rooted in Israel's history. But when we dig deeper with a Christocentric approach, we see that the passage is really and ultimately about Christ. It's about what we need (an offering for atonement via blood). The repeated sacrifices of our spiritual ancestors were hands reaching out for Christ. The passage is also about how we're saved through grace, through a self-giving person who offered himself willingly for those who despised him. And it's also a passage about where our hope lies, our destiny: full atonement means full oneness (at-*one*-ment) with God.[93] This passage is about Christ, and reading it from this perspective helps me to grow deeper in union with him. It draws me to the oneness of fellowship I have with God.

> My Christ, you opened up yourself to me,
> You put your body on the altar.
> And as the redness stained the tree,
> You steadied every falter.
>
> Because of you, my soul is free
> To remain instead of roam,
> To huddle in the Trinity,
> To gather in your home.

Summary

Union with Christ means we open our imagination to living *in* another person, to having a home with hands and feet. Practically speaking, our Spirit-wrought union with Christ means that *his* heart and will become *our* heart and will, a gentle and lowly self-giving.

To go deeper in our union with him, we walk on a path of speech. We trod on God's words, a great, expansive field, knowing that every blade of grass has something to tell us about Christ. We listen. We respond. We worship.

In the next chapter, we'll focus more deeply on cultivating oneness with God in private—using the method I've exemplified above—so that this oneness can change the world in public, in our thought, speech, and action.

Additional Resources for Christ-Centered Interpretation

Clowney, Edmund P. *Preaching Christ in All of Scripture.* Wheaton, IL: Crossway, 2003.

———. *The Unfolding Mystery: Discovering Christ in the Old Testament.* Colorado Springs, CO: NavPress, 1988.

Johnson, Dennis E. *Him We Proclaim: Preaching Christ from All the Scriptures.* Phillipsburg, NJ: P&R, 2007.

Lillback, Peter A., ed. *Seeing Christ in All of Scripture: Hermeneutics at Westminster Theological Seminary.* Glenside, PA: Westminster Seminary Press, 2016.

Poythress, Vern S. *Reading the Word of God in the Presence of God: A Handbook for Biblical Interpretation.* Wheaton, IL: Crossway, 2016 (pp. 233–246).

———. *The Shadow of Christ in the Law of Moses.* Phillipsburg, NJ: P&R, 1995.

Zartmen, Ruben. "How Does Christ 'Fulfill' Historical Remarks?" Reformed Forum, May 9, 2018. https://reformedforum.org/how-does-christ-fulfill-historical-remarks/.

Reflection Questions and Prayer

1. In what ways does union with Christ still seem mysterious to you?

2. We are united *to* a person (Christ) *by* a person (the Spirit). Yet, we often feel distanced from God. Why? (Try to go beyond "sin" as an answer, and think of the theological and practical causes introduced in an earlier chapter.)

3. Tell your story about being united with Christ. Either write it down or describe it to a friend. What has your experience been like *since* that union? How have you seen Christ's heart and will become your own?

4. Does the idea that God is *speaking* to you in Scripture sound strange? If so, why? What do you think prevents people from viewing Scripture as the speech of God to them?

Prayer
My Christ . . . It feels so good to call you mine,

And to know that I am yours.
Spirit, you made my life part of Christ's vine.
I'm in him now, planted and secure.
It all goes beyond my wildest imaginings.
How can I be living *in* another person?
I'll never fully understand it,
But I want to live it.
I want my union with Christ
To keep changing me.
I know I need to speak with you,
To hear your voice and respond.
Help me to truly *live* as if I'm in the presence
Of three divine persons.
Christ, show me your will and heart
For those people and problems I meet today.
Spirit, tell me what to say.
Father, help me trust you.

Reader Resource: Famous Dialogue Starters

In the next chapter, we'll get into what I call *speechpaths*. To prep your mind for that, below are some of the most famous passages of Scripture. Read them now as part of a dialogue, as God speaking to you. Try your best to use the tools from the end of this chapter to arrive at a Christ-centered interpretation.

Then, consider what you might say in response to God. Try to let each passage direct your focus for a whole day.

- Now the Lord said to Abram, "Go from your country and your kindred and your father's house to the land that I will show you. And I will make of you a great nation, and I will bless you and make your name great, so that you will be a blessing. I will bless those who bless you, and him who dishonors you I will curse, and in you all the families of the earth shall be blessed." (Gen. 12:1–3)

- "Hear, O Israel: The Lord our God, the Lord is one. You shall love the Lord your God with all your heart and with all your soul and with all your might. 6 And these words that I command you today shall be on your heart. You shall teach them diligently to your children, and shall talk of them when you sit in your house, and when you walk by the way, and when you lie down, and when you rise. You shall bind them as a sign on your hand, and they shall be as frontlets between your eyes. You shall write them on the doorposts of your house and on your gates. (Deut. 6:4–9)

- Now the boy Samuel was ministering to the Lord in the presence of Eli. And the word of the Lord was rare in those days; there was no frequent vision. At that time Eli, whose eyesight had begun to grow dim so that he could not see, was lying down in his own place. The lamp of God had not yet gone out, and Samuel was lying down in the temple of the Lord, where the ark of God was. Then the Lord called Samuel, and he said, "Here I am!" and ran to Eli and said, "Here I am, for you called me." But he said, "I did not call; lie down again." So he went and lay down. And the Lord called again, "Samuel!" and Samuel arose and went to Eli and said, "Here I am, for you called me." But he said, "I did not call, my son; lie down again." Now Samuel did not yet know the Lord, and the word of the Lord had not yet been revealed to him. And the Lord called Samuel again the third time. And he arose and went to Eli and said, "Here I am, for you called me." Then Eli perceived that the Lord was calling the boy. Therefore Eli said to Samuel, "Go, lie down, and if he calls you, you shall say, 'Speak, Lord, for your servant hears.'" So Samuel went and lay down in his place. And the Lord came and stood, calling as at other times, "Samuel! Samuel!" And Samuel said, "Speak, for your servant hears." (1 Sam. 3:1–10)

- The Lord is my shepherd; I shall not want. He makes me lie down in green pastures. He leads me beside still waters. He restores my soul. He leads me in paths of righteousness for his name's sake. Even though I walk through the valley of the shadow of death, I will fear no evil, for you are with me; your rod and your staff, they comfort me. You prepare a table before me in the presence of my enemies; you anoint my head with oil; my cup overflows. Surely goodness and mercy shall follow me all the days of my life, and I shall dwell in the house of the Lord forever. (Ps. 23)

- Now when Jesus came, he found that Lazarus had already been in the tomb four days. Bethany was near Jerusalem, about two miles off, and many of the Jews had come to Martha and Mary to console them concerning their brother. So when Martha heard that Jesus was coming, she went and met him, but Mary remained seated in the house. Martha said to Jesus, "Lord, if you had been here, my brother would not have died. But even now I know that whatever you ask from God, God will give you." Jesus said to her, "Your brother will rise again." Martha said to him, "I know that he will rise again in the resurrection on the last day." Jesus said to her, "I am the resurrection and the life. Whoever believes in me, though he die, yet shall he live, and everyone who lives and believes in me shall never die. Do you believe this?" She said to him, "Yes, Lord; I believe that you are the Christ, the Son of God, who is coming into the world." (John 11:17–27)

CHAPTER NINE

ONENESS IN PRIVATE

Cultivating Communion

How do you draw near invisible persons? There must be a channel for communication. There must be a way for sharing.

Kenneth Pike was a Christian linguist whose thought has deeply marked my own. He had these mysterious and striking expressions throughout his writings—words that needed to be mined for the treasure they held. Here's one of them: "Sharing is prerequisite to change."[94] If there's going to be communication between persons, if there's going to be communion, something must be shared among them. There has to be some common base on which they stand to communicate. Do you know what that is for us and God? It's the Spirit of God himself. A *person* enables us to commune with God, to be one with him. And because of the power of that person, we know that change is bound to come. In this context, "change" means the aligning of our heart and will with Christ's, the deepening of our union with Christ into the rich, teeming waters of communion, the waters of closeness. Sharing God's Spirit is prerequisite to change in communion, in relationship.

This makes a lot of sense since the Spirit is the one who unites us to Christ. Why would the Spirit *not* abide in order to draw us deeper into oneness?

In this chapter, we're exploring how oneness grows in the quiet greenhouse of our souls. We have to start there if we want the oneness that changes us to have any chance of changing the world. And Jesus was clear that the whole point of our oneness *was* to change the world, that others might know he was sent by the Father. Oneness in private, however, comes before oneness in public. The natural question is, How do we cultivate this oneness in private? We must begin with the truth that sharing is prerequisite to change, that we must have God's Spirit within us if we long to grow closer to him. And we do.

We've already talked about this, so why emphasize it again? For our confidence. Oneness with God, deeper communion with him, isn't just a *possibility* for those united to Christ; it's an *inevitability*. This is the Spirit of the omnipotent God we're talking about! If he's the one working in us to draw us nearer to God, how could we have any doubts that it would happen?

In other words, I'm starting here because we often approach our communion with God in shy hope rather than straight-backed certainty. But we *have* that certainty. We have the Spirit. We are *in* the Son of God. And, as Dane Ortlund put it, "If you are in Christ, you are as eternally invincible as he is."[95] Do we act as if we are invincible? I don't think so. Weak. Brittle. Faithless. Timid. Nonchalant. But not invincible. Why not? We're on a path to oneness with the living, eternal God! We need to start acting invincible. We need to start acting more like victors and less like underdogs. It has *nothing* to do with our own abilities. It has *everything* to do with God's. Let's start there. If you are in Christ and indwelt by the Holy Spirit, oneness is going to deepen.

God invites us into the journey of deeper communion with him. The beauty is in the travel, not just in the destination. And this chapter is about what that travel looks like. Here it is in a snapshot: *a speechpath*. By the end of the chapter, you'll know what that means. And it will have everything to do with your deepening communion with God.

Speechpaths

Edmund Clowney wrote a classic on Christian spirituality: *Christian Meditation: What the Bible Teaches about Meditation and Spiritual Exercises*. As we saw in the previous chapter, deepening oneness with God is going to be a matter of speech (keep the word "speechpath" in mind), and *meditation* on the speech of God is the first step.

What does Christian meditation do? It "reflects on the truth of God in the presence of God."[96] This reflection on God's truth isn't cold fact memorization. It glows like embers of love. Knowing God is loving him; "knowing God and loving God are acts of co mmunion."[97] That's what we're after. That's what we're born for: communion with God, oneness. As our knowledge of God deepens, our *love* is meant to deepen. If it's not deepening, something is off. Knowledge that doesn't lead to deeper love is worthless. Think on that for a moment.

This is where our speechpath begins, with the speech of God in Scripture. When we soak in that speech, we're drawn to deeper love. But this isn't a matter of human effort. It's the Spirit of God working in us. God takes the initiative in the blooming peony of oneness—making us so full and heavy that we must bow down. That's what he's done in loving us. His filling makes us fall in worship. But he came *down* to fill us up with his love. "Love is not the upward ascent of our souls that sublimates us into union with the deity. Rather, love is the descent of God's royal grace that conquers our rebellion, atones for our guilt, and draws us into sonship."[98] Love meets us on the ground to draw us up. It doesn't demand that we rise up in worthiness. In fact, the very heart of God is to draw near with gentleness to those who are broken. This is God. This is love. This is Jesus meek and mild.

Love comes down to help us start walking on our speechpath, our communion trail with the Trinity. The first step on the speechpath is meditating on God's words.

What does that meditation look like? Clowney writes that the three distinctives of Christian meditation are that it's "centered on the truth of God, moved by the love of God, and directed to the praise of God."[99] Let's break these down with an example.

Centered on the Truth

To center is to focus. And focus can be achieved in all sorts of ways. Here are three.

- Repetition
- Slow, thoughtful reading
- Prayerful consideration of meaning

Let's center on Acts 3:1–10. Read it slowly. But *before* you read, pray this prayer: "God, open my eyes to the wild brightness of your truth." Sometimes I offer a simple prayer like that to help my mind focus. Then I read slowly.

> Now Peter and John were going up to the temple at the hour of prayer, the ninth hour. ² And a man lame from birth was being carried, whom they laid daily at the gate of the temple that is called the Beautiful Gate to ask alms of those entering the temple. ³ Seeing Peter and John about to go into the temple, he asked to receive alms. ⁴ And Peter directed his gaze at him, as did John, and said, "Look at us." ⁵ And he fixed his attention on them, expecting to receive something from them. ⁶ But Peter said, "I have no silver and gold, but what I do have I give to you. In the

name of Jesus Christ of Nazareth, rise up and walk!" ⁷ And he took him by the right hand and raised him up, and immediately his feet and ankles were made strong. ⁸ And leaping up, he stood and began to walk, and entered the temple with them, walking and leaping and praising God. ⁹ And all the people saw him walking and praising God, ¹⁰ and recognized him as the one who sat at the Beautiful Gate of the temple, asking for alms. And they were filled with wonder and amazement at what had happened to him.

What captured me as I read were the words "the Beautiful Gate." Here was a man broken and begging, set before a gate whose name must have seemed to mock his legs. His legs were thin and sickly, still as stones. They didn't feel beautiful. But they would soon. And a *name* would make them move. And once they did, then that gate before him would be truly beautiful, for he would go from waiting and watching to *walking*. Gates are meant to be entered. No gate is beautiful if it keeps out those called to walk.

I was also captured by Peter's confident faith, which could only be the power of God's own Spirit in him. "In the name of Jesus Christ of Nazareth, rise up and walk" (3:6). You get a name, a place, and then a command. But the name is king. The name has power. As I paused after reading, I thought, "Your *name* has the power to redeem and restore." That seemed worthy of repetition, so I said it a few times, enough to make it easy to recall throughout the day whenever I stumbled across thoughts, words, and actions in need of redemption and restoration. It became a refrain. "Your *name* has the power to redeem and restore."

"Wonder and amazement" is what the people felt. That's what I felt, too. How could sinew and muscle and blood come to life at the mention of a name? Especially a name used today as a common curse word—something people mutter when they smack their thumb with a hammer. How can a name bring life? I won't try to offer an answer because it would embarrass the power of the almighty. It would be like trying to count the stars. You can begin, but you can't end. I walk away from this passage in wonder with the words, "Your name has the power to redeem and restore." I was centered on that truth.

Moved by the Love of God

After centering on this truth of God, there must be movement beyond the mind. Open-mouthed wonder happens in the head, but what of the heart? The heart needs to drag the head into the river of love. We need to rest in its current, letting it carry us. I have this sentence about God in my head—"Your name has the power to redeem and restore"—but ideas need to be animated and applied by *persons*. Enter the Holy Spirit, the person responsible for my rebirth in Christ.

Spirit, what love comes from this? Love is self-giving. And the Trinity has given us himself in giving us his name. Remember that bit of John 17? "Holy Father, keep them in your name, which you have given me, that they may be one, even as we are one. While I was with them, I kept them in your name, which you have given me" (17:11–12). The name was given to the Son. The Son kept us *in* it. We are given that name as a home. We live in the name that redeems all darkness and restores all that's lost or broken. We live there. And we are *never* going to move out. We are sons and daughters in a home without an end. The *name* of God is *our* beautiful gate. Once we enter, by the grace-dripping hand of a suffering servant God, we remain. We're safe. We're okay. All threats to our good and livelihood are silenced. Not even death can touch us in our name-home. We. Are. Invincible. Remember? We're invincible because of grace, because God is a giver.

My heart is starting to well up with love and gratitude. I have entered the beautiful gate. I have a name-home forever. I'm all set. All because a gentle and lowly savior extended his arms on the cross so that he could draw me into his embrace. The cross is an act of love captured midway. Christ's arms are open not just to pay for sin but to prepare for our embrace. His arms opened up so they could wrap around us. He was stretched in exile so that he could welcome us home. Does that not make you want to sing? Does that not call forth your love, like nectar offering itself through the tiny white tips of clover flowers? Don't you just feel like giving yourself back to the one who gave himself for you? That's love.

Directed to the Praise of God

It's not a long way from love to praise—only a millimeter. Once you're in love, praise pours out. I'm madly in love with my wife.

Our love grows stronger and deeper with time. Do you know how easy and effortless it is for me to sing her praises? To tell others about how beautiful and talented and compassionate she is as a person? Praise hangs on love's coattails. It follows love like a giddy younger sister.

After meditating on Acts 3:1–10, I'm filled with praise for the God who made me a home in his name. That longing to praise can come out in song, but it can also come out in other actions. Praising God is simply shouting his goodness and beauty from the rooftops, calling attention to his meek and mighty love. We can do that in any action that points to God's goodness and beauty—provided we do it with a heart of love.

Putting the dishes away is something I do everyday. It can seem mundane, and often I do it thoughtlessly. But there are moments when I'm filled with praise for what God has been teaching me, like what we just looked at in Acts 3. "Your name has the power to redeem and restore." Putting things in their right place—that sounds a lot like stacking ceramic bowls and plates. My stacking happens in an atmosphere of praise. This is what God does in far more beautiful ways: He sets things where they're supposed to be, separating the clean from the unclean. Doing dishes is priestly work, the work of Christ.

Does anyone notice me doing the dishes this way, smiling as I imagine Christ's hands around my own, putting to right what was soiled and stained? Maybe not, except for God. But isn't he the best audience anyway?

What we just did together is a *speechpath*: centering on God's truth, being moved to love, directed to praise. It's a path of words, cut through the wilds of our experience by the God of speech. This is what we need to cultivate deeper oneness with God. But there are two other components to a speechpath that we can't miss.

Prayer

Part of a speechpath is God speaking to us. The other part is us speaking to God. There is no thriving relationship without dialogue.

Sometimes in Scripture we meet a direct and critical command, a comet in the black sky of our awareness. But unlike a comet, which burns out, these commands are meant to burn on . . . inside us, giving us light and warmth. One of them comes in 1 Thessalonians 5:16–18. It puts in plain terms the will of the almighty, beautiful, mysterious God. Brace yourself.

> "Rejoice always, pray without ceasing, give thanks in all circumstances; for this is the will of God in Christ Jesus for you."

Rejoice because you've been given everything (2 Cor. 6:10). You possess *all*. Do you believe that? In Christ you own everything good and beautiful. In him, you have it all. And you can't ever lose it. So start with a smile. Start with rejoicing.

Then pray . . . *without ceasing*. Don't be content with a five-minute quiet time. Talk to God throughout the day. In line at the grocery store. Standing at the gas pump. In between pushes as your child swings at the park. While petting your dog. In between coffee swigs. Make prayer a reflex—both for troubles and for triumphs, for heart breaks and hallelujahs. Prayer should be a reflex, not a last resort.

If this sounds too intimidating, then start by focusing on *listening*. We forget that prayer isn't just our speech to God; it's our listening for God's voice in the quietness. It's always happening, but we aren't always listening. Adam McHugh writes,

> When we enter into prayer, no matter what the circumstances, we step into a conversation that has been happening since the foundation of the world but is now happening not only apart from us but *through* us. The Spirit groans in us, the Son intercedes in us, the Father listens to us. We have been drawn into the heart of trinitarian conversation. Our existence has become an enfleshed, walking conversation.[100]

Sometimes we have such a hard time speaking in prayer that we forget about the centrality of listening. Listening is perhaps an even greater component of prayer than speaking. And McHugh goes as far as to say, "I see no other way that we can be faithful to Paul's injunction to 'pray without ceasing' unless we understand prayer as listening and all of life as the context for listening prayer."[101]

But whether we're speaking or listening, we'll have a lot of mind-cleaning to do. Once we start to pray, Satan sets up his archers. Their quivers are loaded with every distraction. Remember those 262 phone checks a day? That comes in here. So do those shirts you were meaning to order. That Taylor Swift song. The absence of a taste in your mouth (what should you eat?). The oil on your face (did you shower today?). The constant checking of time and weather. Arrow after arrow. Satan's aim is to draw you out of Godtalk. And he's good at it . . . *really* good.

But not good enough. Remember that the Spirit of the one who keeps the stars blazing and the ocean temperature steady—he lives inside you, with Christ and the Father. You are a house for God. Say it out loud. "I am a house for God." The devil's distractions can't win the day because God already has. And he planted himself inside you. Keep praying, and ask for the Spirit's power to burn away the haze of distractions. With some mind-cleaning and persistence, you'll get there. We all will. Because God has already won your soul for himself. And he prayed for your oneness with him.

And that should lead to thanksgiving in all circumstances. Does it for you? Many times, when our circumstances are poor, we stare at them. Rather than seeing them as tools being wielded for our good, we see them as cuts that are sapping our spirits, letting out our lifeblood and drawing us into darkness. We don't give thanks; we give griping. We embrace self-pity. We pick up the shiny coin of jealousy and turn it over in our palms.

Giving thanks is bound up with something we discussed at the outset of this book: contentment in Christ. That's how Paul was able to focus on his relationship with God and not his horrendous circumstances. That's how he was able to be a mountain climber. And that's how we'll be steadfast climbers as well. In fact, Paul was content not just *despite* his circumstances but *with* his circumstances. That's a huge difference. Sinclair Ferguson writes,

> Only when our Christ is big enough to satisfy us can we be content no matter our particular circumstances; more than that, satisfied *with* the circumstances and not merely *despite* the circumstances. This is a telling point. We have not yet attained to biblical contentment when we would be content with Christ were it not for our circumstances. No, genuine contentment is realized both *in* our circumstances and *with* our circumstances.[102]

What does he mean here? If we're content *with* our circumstances, that means we see them as tools for Christ-conformity. The tough things we encounter aren't obstacles to be avoided; they're tools to be used.[103] Think of difficult things as utensils for shaping and marking clay. They emboss and inscribe, burnish and carve, remove and reveal. What are they revealing? The image of Christ to whom we're being shaped! And that's the best thing that could ever happen to a human being, that we would look more and more like the Son of God! God is using everything. Everything.

As a kid, I always loved hearing about how Native Americans who hunted buffalo would use *every* piece of the animal for their livelihood. Meat for food; skins for shelter and clothing and moccasins, bones for tools; hooves to make glue; horns for digging sticks; the bladder for a cooking utensil; even the dung for fuel. Everything was used. Nothing was wasted, no matter how vile that seems to us. Something like this resembles what God does with our trials and difficulties, our hard things. They seem repulsive and disgusting to us, unclean and barbaric. We don't even want to touch them or be in their presence, let alone *use* them. But God doesn't waste anything. In fact, God is a craftsman with our crushing experiences. He takes what's hideous and puts it to work for his good purposes.

In Andrew Peterson's brilliant series *The Wingfeather Saga*, there is an evil lord called Gnag the Nameless. He's responsible for torturing and even mutilating some of the creatures in their world, creatures made by "the Maker." One of the characters, Artham Wingfeather, who was changed by evil forces but then goes through a process of redemption, stands before an angry mob and declares how the Maker works. "Gnag bends things for breaking, and the Maker makes a flourish! Evil digs a pit, and the Maker makes a well! That is his way."[104] This is a reflection of how God works in our own lives. When we believe in that (and it always takes the Spirit's help to do it), we can start to be content *with* our circumstances, not *despite* them. Our pits will turn to wells

Ferguson also lays out five dimensions of our contentment in Christ. Each of these seems clearly linked to prayer.[105]

- "Everything we need and everything we lack is found in Christ."

- "This all-sufficient Christ is with us."

- "We are in this all-sufficient Christ."

- "This all-sufficient Christ is in us."

- We have not yet "attained to its full realization."

We pray in the Spirit that God would help us see our every need and longing fulfilled in the *person* given for us. We pray that we'd be constantly reminded of Christ's presence. We pray that we think and live as if we're truly *in* Christ, and that he truly lives *in* us. And we pray with hope and longing for the day when we'll be fully united with him. These are things we should be praying for everyday. They're truths we should voice in meditation and then listen for God's response, even in the form of silence.

But we struggle to pray for them once a week, or even once a month, don't we? We're still plagued by self-sufficiency syndrome, drawn down to the earth with worldly cares and aspirations, our feet booted with lead, our wings lacking the plumage we need to soar on the thermals of grace. But God never gives up on us. He works until we fly with him in eternity. The expanse is our home. Don't forget it.

Now, if we're truly and deeply content in Christ, if we really believe that we possess *everything* in him, then all else is extra. Every breath. Every finger movement. Every taste. Every sound. Every conversation. Every safe commute to work. Every breakfast. It's all gift.

Our trouble is that we treat these everyday *gifts* as *rights*. We act as if they aren't extra; they're the minimum requirement. They're the lowest bar. We *should* get all these things. We *deserve* them, don't we?

The issue with this mindset isn't just that it's ungrateful. The deeper issue is that it reveals what we really think about Christ, about possessing all in him. It reveals either that we don't fully believe that we possess all in him, or it reveals that, in our hearts, we don't think that's enough. We want *Christ—and*, not just Christ.

Can you see how problematic this is? If having the Son of God and every spiritual blessing running over into eternity isn't enough, then what is?

I think the spiritual response to this is a matter of digging. We need to take a spade to our heart-soil. What's beneath the surface? Is it disbelief (the gospel *does* seem too good to be true)? Is it lesser loves (materialism, health, relationships, egoism)? Why are those lesser loves so gripping for us? Dig. Go at least three layers of *why* into your heart. I'll give you an example.

I don't fully believe I possess all in Christ. *Why?* Because my definition of "all" includes material comforts.

Why? Because that's what I can experience right now, and I like that.

Why? Because I don't fully believe that I'll live forever with Christ. I think this life is all I've got.

Woah. There's some revelation. Being candid in going three levels deep will show you what's taking root beneath the heart-soil. Healing starts with honesty. So, dig. And be honest. And then? Pray some more. You'll know what to ask for . . . or what to listen for.

Obedience

The final part of the speechpath isn't what you'd expect. It's an action. But apart from obedient, Spirit-ignited action, oneness with God can't blossom. There will still be a gap between you. If oneness with God means aligning your heart and will with his, then your will has to lead to God-honoring action.

This doesn't mean that you and I work our way into oneness, as if it were all up to us. We're citizens of Grace Country. Our history and heritage stand on the open hands of God, not on the grasping attempts of self. Obedience isn't an attempt to earn oneness, a loving fellowship with the relational God. We've already been given that fellowship. But we keep ourselves from experiencing it more fully because of a strange identity crisis.

We think, like the rest of the world, that our identity is being carved one day at a time, one chisel chip tumbling away from our marble base each moment we do or experience something. Every thought, every word, every action is another chip. Each day we're taking shape, defining our length and breadth and depth, adding curves and rolling muscle. Each day, we keep making ourselves. This all sounds so natural that it's hard to remember it's biblically false. Let me say it again: We do not define our identity day by day.

The radical, revealed truth for us in Scripture is this: *Our identity is already defined.* All the contours and curves, the structure and serene beauty, is there. We are *already* Michelangelo's *David*. We're just covered with sand. The sand drifts away in the wind of the Spirit as we stare at the one to whom we bear divine family resemblance.

Wilbourne put it this way:

> When I base my Christian life on my Christian experience, I become locked in the labyrinth of my own performance. I am only as sure of God as my current emotions and obedience allow. My eyes are fixed on myself. The gospel, the good news, is the way the Holy Spirit turns our eyes away from ourselves and onto Christ. The gospel brings you into union with Christ. Christ enters your heart and gives you faith. By that faith you receive Christ and all his fullness. Faith fixes your eyes on Christ and rests in him.[106]

Note the paradox of "fixing" and "resting." We're *both* active through the Spirit and passive in our person-given identity.

We participate *and* receive. The reception means Michelangelo's *David* is already finished. The participation means we get to show up and watch the sand clear away from that breath-taking figure. Obedience is showing up. It's participating in the divine bestowal of our Christ-framed identity. When we don't show up, our identity isn't absent; it's just waiting for us. We can't see all of it with the sand surrounding it, but it's there. We are already our truest selves in Christ.

Listen to the way Paul describes our daily life. "For we are his workmanship, created in Christ Jesus for good works, which God prepared beforehand, that we should walk in them" (Eph. 2:10).

First, notice that we're not ultimately working on ourselves; *God* is working on us. We are *his* workmanship. Second, our identity is in another. We are created *in* Christ Jesus. As we saw earlier, our identity is not a "me"; it's an "us."[107] But, third, look at what that identity has for a purpose: good works. When we are most ourselves, we're bent towards the goodness of God. But this doesn't mean we blaze our own path, much to the chagrin of contemporary culture. God has already prepared the path. He's marked the trail. We just have to walk.

What will that look like? It will look like love. It will look like self-giving. It will look gentle and lowly. The poet Christian Wiman described love like this:

> Love, which awakens our souls and to which we cling
> like the splendid mortal creatures that we are, asks
> us to let it go, to let it be more than it is if it is *only*

us. To manage this highest form of loving does not mean that we will be showered with earthly delights or somehow be spared awful human suffering. But for as long as we can live in this sacred space of receiving and releasing, and can learn to speak and to be love's fluency, then the greater love that is God brings a continuous and enlarging air into our existence. We feel love leave us in unthreatening ways. We feel it reenter us at once more truly and more strange, like a simple kiss that has a bit of starlight to it.[108]

Sometimes that's what I want most—a continuous and enlarging air for my identity, the way it felt when I bought my father that little glass guitar. I want to not feel so trapped by my own vanity and short-sightedness, to have the sand cleared away from my God-given, Christ-conformed, Spirit-infused identity. To have more space in which to *be*.

Obedience makes the space. It clears the sand. It lets us thrive in the holy and eternal atmosphere of who we really are by the grace of God. The end of every speechpath, of every act of hearing and speaking with God, is obedience—not because we should "do the right thing" but because the right thing is *us*. It's who we are already in Christ. And we can't draw nearer to God, we can't enjoy deeper oneness with him, if we're constantly pretending to be someone else, someone lesser, someone less like the Christ in whom we were created for good works.

Obedience, in this sense, isn't an application we make after studying God's word. It's the revealing of who we already are in Jesus by grace! And when we are most ourselves, when the sand has been swept away around our Christ-carved identity, there is nothing in between us and God. The gap closes. We are most one with God when our heart and will align with his, revealing our grace-given selves. Obedience isn't something you do; it's something you *are* in Christ, and that secured, established identity is being uncovered right now. Every day. Every moment. With each word you read and thought you think. Obedience means God is helping you see who you *are* in him.

Combining this with what we learned about Christ-centered interpretation in the last chapter, we have the following graphic.

Speechpath

GOD'S WORD Always about Christ
  Centered on the truth
  Moved by love
  Directed to praise

PRAYER
  Rejoice
  Pray constantly
  Give thanks
  Listen

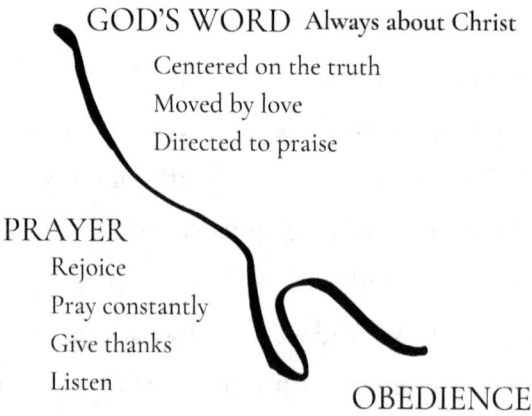

OBEDIENCE

Before we end the chapter, let me remind you of a commonly forgotten truth about obedience: *Obedience is about hope*. We don't usually think of it that way, do we? We think of obedience as being about authority or fear of punishment or stoic resolution. But hope?

In reflecting on Psalm 132, Eugene Peterson wrote, "Obedience is fulfilled by hope."[109] We obey not simply because of what we're called to do in the present but because of the hope that's calling *to* us from the future. Obedience is as much a forward-looking act as it is a backwards-looking one. When we obey, of course, we look at the past, at what God has said and done and commanded. But we rarely look forward. We rarely ask, "What is the future going to look like if I obey?" And that's a shame, because the future would give us so much encouragement. Do you know what's in that future? A more authentic, Christ-resembling portrait of yourself. A you that's closer to God. A you that finds more joy and satisfaction in his presence than in anything else. We obey because we hope in that. And that hope will never be in vain. Obey with hope. Not with irritation or disappointment or self-pity, but with *hope*. God is making you beautiful.

Oneness with God is cultivated in private through our speech-paths, our daily acts of listening, speaking, and obeying. The most extraordinary reality we have access to—oneness with the almighty, three-personed, life-giving Spirit—blooms in this ordinary practice. The gradual process does nothing to diminish the beauty. A white rose on a trellis is no less beautiful for having taken weeks to sprout and climb and bloom. Little by little, moment by moment, speechpath by speechpath, oneness grows.

Reflection Questions and Prayer

1. What obstacles might you face in trying to develop a particular speechpath?

2. What dangers will Christians face in trying to interpret a passage of Scripture?

3. Which part of the speechpath do you find most challenging (centered on the truth, moved to the love of God, directed to the praise of God)?

4. Go three levels deep with a *why* question concerning your response to your riches in Christ. What do you find?

Prayer
My holy speaker,
You're always addressing me.
Your words in Scripture call for response,
But my heart can be dull;
It can see your words as ideas,
Rather than living speech.
Awaken me to the living wonder
Of your words.

Help me to hear your voice,
To wait for your words
To resound in me
And then to respond.
Spirit, give me my speech path for this day.
And help me to walk it every hour.

Reader Resource: Speechpath Starters

The previous chapter had some of the most common passages of Scripture as speechpath starters. Here are some less well-known passages that I've found helpful. What other passages would you add to the list? The important thing to remember is that *every* passage of Scripture can be a speechpath, and every speechpath will lead you deeper into Christ, into higher rooms in the castle of his person.

- Now a man from the house of Levi went and took as his wife a Levite woman. [2] The woman conceived and bore a son, and when she saw that he was a fine child, she hid him three months. [3] When she could hide him no longer, she took for him a basket made of bulrushes and daubed it with bitumen and pitch. She put the child in it and placed it among the reeds by the river bank. [4] And his sister stood at a distance to know what would be done to him. [5] Now the daughter of Pharaoh came down to bathe at the river, while her young women walked beside the river.

She saw the basket among the reeds and sent her servant woman, and she took it. ⁶ When she opened it, she saw the child, and behold, the baby was crying. She took pity on him and said, "This is one of the Hebrews' children." ⁷ Then his sister said to Pharaoh's daughter, "Shall I go and call you a nurse from the Hebrew women to nurse the child for you?" ⁸ And Pharaoh's daughter said to her, "Go." So the girl went and called the child's mother. ⁹ And Pharaoh's daughter said to her, "Take this child away and nurse him for me, and I will give you your wages." So the woman took the child and nursed him. ¹⁰ When the child grew older, she brought him to Pharaoh's daughter, and he became her son. She named him Moses, "Because," she said, "I drew him out of the water." (Exod. 2:1–10)

- ¹⁰ "If any one of the house of Israel or of the strangers who sojourn among them eats any blood, I will set my face against that person who eats blood and will cut him off from among his people. ¹¹ For the life of the flesh is in the blood, and I have given it for you on the altar to make atonement for your souls, for it is the blood that makes atonement by the life. ¹² Therefore I have said to the people of Israel, No person among you shall eat blood, neither shall any stranger who sojourns among you eat blood. ¹³ "Any one also of the people of Israel, or of the strangers who sojourn among them, who takes in hunting any beast or bird that may be eaten shall pour out its blood and cover it with earth. ¹⁴ For the life of every creature is its blood: its blood is its life. Therefore I have said to the people of Israel, You shall not eat the blood of any creature, for the life of every creature is its blood. (Lev. 17:10–14)

- ¹⁷ Deal bountifully with your servant, that I may live and keep your word. ¹⁸ Open my eyes, that I may behold wondrous things out of your law. ¹⁹ I am a sojourner on the earth; hide not your commandments from me! ²⁰ My soul is consumed with longing for your rules at all times. ²¹ You rebuke the insolent, accursed ones, who wander from your commandments. ²² Take away from me scorn and contempt, for I have kept your testimonies. ²³ Even though princes sit plotting against me, your servant will meditate on your statutes. ²⁴ Your testimonies are my delight; they are my counselors. (Ps. 119:17–24)

- Now there was a man of the Pharisees named Nicodemus, a ruler of the Jews. ² This man came to Jesus by night and said to him, "Rabbi, we know that you are a teacher come from God, for no one can do these signs that you do unless God is with him." ³ Jesus answered him, "Truly, truly, I say to you, unless one is born again he cannot see the kingdom of God." ⁴ Nicodemus said to him, "How can a man be born when he is old? Can he enter a second time into his mother's womb and be born?" ⁵ Jesus answered,

"Truly, truly, I say to you, unless one is born of water and the Spirit, he cannot enter the kingdom of God. 6 That which is born of the flesh is flesh, and that which is born of the Spirit is spirit. 7 Do not marvel that I said to you, 'You must be born again.' 8 The wind blows where it wishes, and you hear its sound, but you do not know where it comes from or where it goes. So it is with everyone who is born of the Spirit." 9 Nicodemus said to him, "How can these things be?" 10 Jesus answered him, "Are you the teacher of Israel and yet you do not understand these things? 11 Truly, truly, I say to you, we speak of what we know, and bear witness to what we have seen, but you do not receive our testimony. 12 If I have told you earthly things and you do not believe, how can you believe if I tell you heavenly things? 13 No one has ascended into heaven except he who descended from heaven, the Son of Man. 14 And as Moses lifted up the serpent in the wilderness, so must the Son of Man be lifted up, 15 that whoever believes in him may have eternal life. (John 3:1–15)

Chapter Ten

ONENESS IN PUBLIC

Oneness with God is communal. Jesus prayed that we would be one with him and the Father—that *we* (plural) would be one. So, as we're cultivating oneness with God in private, it has to have public consequences. It has to mean something to someone other than us. It has to serve others. As we near the end of the book, we need to think about the power of oneness that goes well beyond us. There are two dimensions: inside the people of God and outside the people of God.

Inside the People of God

Our oneness with God scorns the thought of individualism. It's not just about "me and Jesus." Jesus is the savior of multitudes, and he holds the door open for the Spirit to enter into hearts unnumbered. If you're one with *this* God, you're one with his church, with his people.

Sinclair Ferguson wrote, "The kind of unity Jesus envisages is patterned after the personal, mutual indwelling of the Father and the Son ('as you, Father, are in me, and I in you,' John 17:21). Just as the Father and Son live together in the fellowship of the Spirit, so, since every believer is indwelt by that same Spirit, our fellowship begins to mirror Theirs."[110] Ours. Theirs. Stare at the plurals for a moment. Oneness for God is a matter of three divine persons. Oneness for us is a matter of legions, joined to their three-personed Lord. Oneness with God ripples into our relationships with his people.

What does this look like? I'll give you four words: *prayer, worship, service,* and *fellowship.*

Prayer

What did the Son of God do in establishing our oneness with God? Many things! Chief among them is his atoning sacrifice and resurrection. But what came before all that? Prayer. He *prayed* for our oneness. Do you pray regularly for the people in your church, the people with whom you are one in Christ? Many do, and we can make it a regular practice since prayer is part of our daily speechpaths. But if we don't, it's like forgetting we have fingers. We're part of one body (1 Cor. 12:12–27), standing on the timeless light of one Spirit. And as Paul wrote, you can't disassemble the body. One part can't live in isolation from the others. It *can't.* If we're not in the habit of praying for our brothers and sisters daily, we're forgetting essential parts of *ourselves*—forgetting our own fingers or feet or femur. We'll be limping. We can't be *of* God's people without praying *for* God's people.

Worship

Worship has great power to unite souls. Francis Chan writes, "Our lack of praise may actually be the biggest cause of our divisions. Once we stop worshiping, all hope for unity is lost. This is what unites us: we can't stop talking about the treasure we have in Jesus. . . . Worship is our path to unity."[111] Yes, worship is our path. Union *with* Christ is our path to oneness with God; worship *of* Christ is our path to oneness with each other. We unite with our brothers and sisters in Christ and sing. In joining our voices, we join our souls. In joining our souls, we unite with the God who saved us. Worship isn't a Sunday morning task; it's a Sunday morning path. Walk it to oneness.

Service

We are one with the person who had everything and yet gave everything away. Jesus said, "The Son of man came not to be served but to serve, and to give his life as a ransom for many" (Mark 10:45). In serving other members of the body of Christ, we proclaim self-awareness *as* one body. Anyone who cares for himself will look after the needs of his body. The church is no different. It should pulse with servitude. They shouldn't have to beg for volunteers to teach Sunday school; they should have to turn people away because service was so prodigally offered.

Service is self-care, and our new self is communal. *You* are *they*.

Fellowship

The sweet gathering of saints just to enjoy moments and minutes in the presence of sinners saved—that's fellowship. Prayer says, "What can I lift up for you?" Worship says, "What can we lift up for *him*?" Service says, "What can I lift for you?" But fellowship says, "How can we have fun lifting each other up?" Though fellowship isn't always instinctive for introverts such as myself, it goes beyond compulsion and into invitation. Surrounding ourselves with like-minded believers does something for our unity. It reminds us that we are living *into* something greater, that time is a foretaste of eternity, that love—from God, in Christ, by the Spirit, for us—cannot die. And since death is the great spiritual threat to life, that's no small thing. Christian Wiman said, "Human love has an end, which is God, who makes it endless."[112] We need reminders and rehearsals of that endless love in the present.

This is counterintuitive for many of us, since we view the passing of time as a loss worthy of melancholy. We treat memories as beautiful paintings lost forever behind the thick glass of the past. But that's not how God sees memory. All throughout Scripture, God calls his people to remember as a source of strength and faith, not melancholy. Memory, paradoxically, drives us forward in faith-filled action, not backwards in waning joy. Memory is not the smoke lost to the sky; it's the light ahead of us in a darkened wood. It's behind us *and* ahead of us. We look backwards so that we can see its golden orb ahead of us, even brighter than we expected. Human love, safe in the arms of God, goes forever. Our little pockets of fellowship with each other are reminders—potent pointers to what lies ahead.

Oneness within the body of Christ looks like prayer, worship, service, and fellowship. Where is your soul wanting in these places? Because our oneness with each other is born from our oneness with God, we can problem solve by going backwards. A lack of prayer for others usually reflects a lack of prayerful communion with God. A lack of passion to worship with others usually reflects a lack of joy and love for the beautiful character of God. A lack of service for others may reflect a lack of self-giving to God in private. And a lack of fellowship may betray a lack of quiet, joyful devotion to God when no one else is around. Study yourself. Pray to the Spirit. He will work. He always does.

Outside the People of God

Jesus makes it very clear in John 17 that our oneness has an evangelistic purpose: "so that the world may believe that you have sent me" (v. 21). Oneness isn't just a possession of the church; it's a power to grow the church. The whole point of our oneness is for the belief of others outside the church.

This is tied to our union with Christ and our Spirit-empowered Christ conformity. Being in Jesus means looking more like Jesus (gentle and lowly self-giving). Looking more like Jesus will have one of two effects: (1) it will draw others toward us as the Spirit stirs them for love of undying beauty, or (2) it will repel others from us for hatred of Christ. "If the world hates you, know that it has hated me" (John 15:18).

But here's the discouraging news: hatred isn't a failsafe measure of your Christlikeness. You can be hated because you resemble Christ, and then you can be hated because you're a self-righteous, judgmental, and insensitive jerk. There's a big difference. Francis Chan puts it more bluntly. "The world currently hates us not because we resemble Jesus but because we don't."[113] That stings. And it should.

Here's the hard part for Westernized, winning-infatuated Christians: *Christ was a loser.* I mean that in the best possible sense. Christ, to every casual eye in his own society, looked as if he was a loser. He wasn't at the top of the religious leadership (actually, they wanted to kill him). He didn't have wealth. He wasn't influential over the broader culture—at least, not during his earthly life. Christ was a loser to the world. That means if you look like him, if you're one with him and with his people, *you* will look like a loser, too.

Now, here's the good news. Christ only *looked* like a loser from the world's perspective. In his Father's eyes, he was the victor in the greatest war of all time. He defeated sin and death! He won over *all*. He overcame the world (John 16:33). It makes me think of wrestling. In his death and resurrection, Christ pinned the world on its back.

Why is this so critical for our oneness with God as a public testament? The Christ to whom we are drawing others is other-worldly. He was *sent*, as John harps on throughout his Gospel, from somewhere else. Victory in union with him will *not* look like victory to our world. It will look like loss, like gentle and lowly self-giving.

In America, there is a huge problem with this. John Piper addressed it in a sermon entitled "The Plundering of Your Property and the Power of Hope." American Christians, because of the prosperity they've enjoyed since the founding of the country, seem to think that Christians should look like winners, that we're at the top, a beacon of moral light for others, that people should feel privileged to have us in their midst. That's *not* a representation of Jesus gentle and lowly. That actually bears a striking resemblance to the Pharisees of Jesus's own day. But the Pharisees, in Jesus's words, were "white-washed tombs, which outwardly appear beautiful, but within are full of dead people's bones and all uncleanness" (Matt. 23:27–28). Following this logic, if you think you should look like a winner in American Christianity, you may be living like a dead person. On the outside, on the surface, American Christians seem confident and "in the right." That's one of the many reasons conservative Christians have confused authentic biblical faith with political affiliations. They're working with the wrong model. They're seeing Christ as a winner in the world's eyes, and so they believe Christianity should "win the day." Mark my words,

Christians will "win the day" precisely when they lose it, when they align their heart and will with the heart and will of Christ, who lost all in this world in order to gain life in the fullest. If your goal and passion is to be one with Christ, with the Trinity, in order to be a testament to God's sending of his Son, that's going to look like loss in the eyes of the world.

But the nature of that loss takes the form of unchecked self-giving, just as Jesus "did not count equality with God a thing to be grasped, but emptied himself, by taking the form of a servant" (Phil. 2:6–7). The loss that we embrace as Christians is a loss of *self*. And in that loss of self lies the light of God's sending. The light of eternity broke through the gray clouds of time in God's self-giving, the giving of his Son. "For God so loved the world, he *gave*" (John 3:16). Our God-like loss is a gift of self.

So Loved
God so loved the world that he *gave*,
Embraced our spinning sphere,
Bound up the planet in Spirit-gauze
And gave us ears to hear.

His voice came in a person small,
A little carpenter for men.
A little life, poured out for all,
A little hope for our amen.

In a shadow, up we grow,

Quiet as a prayer,
Toward a palace bathed in light,
Shedding every earthly care.

Until the light falls on our face,
We give out every breath,
A gift that shows God's chase
Beyond the door of death.

If we want to be a testimony to Christ, if we want to beckon brothers and sisters to the light and life of God, we must resemble the God who *gave* himself. *That's* when onlookers will pause and say, "Why aren't they trying to hold onto the things we're all after?" Because we count *all* as loss apart from Christ, knowing him in his life, death, and resurrection, communing with him now.

Reflection Questions and Prayer

1. In what ways have you seen your communion with God be a testimony for others?

2. Choose one of the manifestations of oneness in public (prayer, worship, service, and fellowship). Which one is most difficult for you and why?

3. What are some different ways in which you could give yourself to others as a testament to your oneness with God?

Prayer
God, the world is watching.
I'm not aware of it often enough.
I think I'm on my own.
But people are watching.
They may not even know it,
But they're looking at what I have,
At this professed "faith."
Is it a façade, or is it real?
Is the thing I'm chasing
Worth life and death?
Spirit, burn in me.
Help me to act on power of your presence.
And let my love and worship of you
In the smallest of things
Draw more attention   To your person-shaping love.

Chapter Eleven

THE DAY ETERNAL

We're almost finished. So, I want to end with something very close to my heart. My father's early death has marked me more deeply than any other life experience. It swept away the shoddy tent of my little teenage world and gave me something bigger. Much bigger. It's hard to describe, but it felt as if the world grew larger every day after his death, and I grew smaller.

That intersects with oneness by highlighting its distance from us, its completion. I want to see my father again. I want him to hear me call him "dad." I want to feel his arms wrap around my back. But I can't yet. Not yet. I have to live with the absence. I have to live with a hole in my heart, letting the ivy of other love cover its surface. The hole remains. I just don't see or feel it all the time.

Our hearts have holes in them. But holes are places where echoes live. We hear them at the backs of our mind, on the fringes of consciousness. We hear echoes.

Some are more recent than others—like my father's voice. But ancient ones are harder to hear. They are the whispers of destiny, of purpose, of transcendence. They call us out of the immediate. They make us wonder about who we really are, where we're going, and how we'll get there. They offer an ancient and epic hope. It's so hard to hear that hope sometimes, isn't it? We get lost in the particulars of the day—the way our clothes fit, the taste of food, the sweat on our face and the oil on our skin. Epic hope becomes an epic fairy tale. We tell ourselves stories about it, but do we really believe it? Do we live *into* it?

I'll be blunt with you: The epic hope that belongs to oneness with God won't sprout or flower apart from our daily response to the ancient echo. We won't know who we truly are apart from conversations with our maker. We won't trust in where we're going if we don't keep hearing about our destination. And we'll feel lost on the way without regular words with God. Oneness with God is both a grace-given reality for us *and* a Spirit-driven travel. In Christ, we are one with the Father, by the power and presence of the Holy Spirit. But in Christ, we're called deeper into oneness through the same Spirit that gives us life. Right now.

We're always, always in desperate need of oneness. It's what we were made for. It's what we most long for as relational creatures made in the image of the relational God. The disease of humanity, of sin, is secretly believing that we're okay on our own. As long as we hold that lie close to our chest, we won't be able to tunnel deeper into the truth, to hear the ancient echo of our destiny and purpose.

In a conversation with one of my brothers, I said that I believed the good and beautiful moments we had with our father growing up weren't lost. They would be saved and stored somehow, kept safe. There would be a great day in which the love and beauty of those moments would live with all of their sound and color: a day eternal.

I think about that eternal day, how I'm adding my own moments to it, even as I stare out at it like a star in the sky. It seems so far away, but the light . . . it still reaches us.

Oneness with God and with each other is the sunshine of that eternal day. We will one day see everything in and through it. We'll bask in it. It will be our embrace, the atmosphere we breathe in. And we will feel whole, satisfied, safe, seen, and loved.

If that sounds too good to be true, then you're thinking of it rightly. It *should* feel that way, given where we stand and sit and sleep right now. It's still a star in the sky. And stars don't appear any closer just because we long to close the distance. The stars stay. We are the ones who move.

When you close this book, the world will keep spinning. You'll go back to the ordinary. You'll pick up a fork. You'll watch a screen. You'll stand and sit and walk and sleep. Life will keep giving you its rhythms. We keep the beat without trying most of the time, that heart beat of the spirit.

What I hope you will carry with you from now on is this.

You were made for oneness; it is who you were and are.
And nothing else in this swollen world will take you very far.
Some things will shimmer bold and call out for both your hands.
But as they drop between your fingers, you'll start to understand.
Our lives are running over with color, sound, and touch.
As we run upon the clovers, does communion matter much?
It does, both now and after, since we're born for God and others.
Hid beneath our treaded clovers lies a God who's thinly covered.
It's the clovered God who speaks in the pages of book.
His voice is stitched to symbols for our fingers on the surface.
Christ walks off every page, when we wouldn't think to look.
Further up and further in we go in our spoken purpose.

The Son of God prayed for our oneness. And his prayers are perfect, efficacious to eternity. While we rest on that, we desperately need a daily practice of oneness to transform our faith, to make us resemble our older brother, who wrote our salvation already, with ink we can't erase. Until we see his face, follow your speechpaths. We'll find ourselves one day at the same great home.

EPILOGUE

Bringing It All Together

Ever since I've begun writing books, I've been told to have an "elevator pitch" for the book. That's been helpful, since people often have an attention span of about fifteen seconds after they ask, "What's it about?" So, here's the elevator pitch if someone asks you what you've been reading: Oneness with God defines who we are (made for communion), why we're here (to testify to the sending of God's Son), and where we're going (to be one with the Trinity in paradise).

Identity

You and I are creatures made for relationship, to be one with the God who is one with himself. That's not just a facet of our identity; it's the heart of it. The God of relationship has called us into relationship with himself. That's why Jesus prays for us to be one with him and the Father (and the Spirit) in John 17. It's who we are, not just what we do. Our very being is constituted by the longing we have for communion with the eternal God. Oneness with God defines who we are.

Purpose

But what are we doing here in a broken world? And what are we supposed to be doing to cultivate the oneness we so deeply need, that yearning we can feel in our marrow? Our purpose is to deepen in our oneness with God so that we can serve as a testimony. People need to know why we're here. And they're watching. What are we chasing after? And why? Those are the unspoken questions lying behind many of the little conversations we have each day.

I always found it fascinating that God wanted the world to know that he had sent his Son (John 17:21). That's the missional purpose of our oneness with God. Why does God want the world to know that he sent his Son? Because that means not only that God can reach us, but that he wants to. He's at the door, waiting in goodwill for us to knock.

I think many of us continue to struggle to really believe in God's immanence, his closeness. God still seems like a distant dream, just beyond the reaches of our awareness, at the cusp of hope. But God wants the world to know he sent for us. In fact, he loves us enough to come in person, and then to give his person for his people.

That's a message the world needs to keep hearing. For God so loved the world that he sent. Our purpose in life is to go deeper in oneness with God so that onlookers marvel. "Could the invisible, all-powerful Spirit who made the world really send himself to us? Why? Why would he even want to do that?" Therein lies the beautiful mystery of love. Love is before, beneath, above, and beyond all explanation, because love originates in God himself. The beautiful message of love, of God sending himself to the lost, needs repeating. And the repeating comes through, among other things, our oneness with God, our constant striving for fellowship with him. Oneness with God is our purpose for living. In a world groaning for redemption, it's why we're here.

Destiny

And oneness with God is also where we're headed. John Owen spoke of our communion with God being "initial and incomplete." We feel the weight of those words. You feel them right now, don't you? I certainly do. I feel the incompleteness when I chase after other things and end up dissatisfied. I feel it when I lose my temper and offer ridicule rather than the hope of change. I feel it when I see the cigarette dangling from the lips of the garbage collector as he empties another can into the back of the truck, glancing at me and nodding. Does he know God in Christ? If not, where is his life heading right now? If my destiny is perfect oneness with God, then what's his substitute, his counterfeit for communion?

I know where I'm going. I'm going to a country of oneness, the journey to which has already been prayed for by the Son of God. Jesus spoke to the Father about this very thing, in the power of the Spirit. And when God speaks to God, change courses into our lives.

So, there you have it. Oneness with God defines who we are (made for communion), why we're here (to testify to the sending of God's Son), and where we're going (to be one with the Trinity in paradise). Puzzling how such a simple number can house so much truth.

Chasing after oneness with God is the most life-altering, soul-shaping, heart-filling thing we can do with our lives. I hope this little book has made that much clear, and that it's set you up to walk the path to oneness with renewed vigor.

I'll see you when we get there.

Thanks so much for reading this book! I consider reading an act of love. In turning these pages, you've been loving me, and I have gratitude for you and the time you've taken. So, thank you.

I'm a firm believer that if a book means something to you, the biggest blessing you can give to the author is to post a short review of it. If this book has helped you in your walk with the Lord, would you consider leaving a short, honest review on Amazon, Barnes & Noble, or another site? And tell at least one other person what the book has done for you. Word of mouth will always be the best way to spread the word about books we value.

Lastly, I'd love to connect with you more regularly. Come and visit my website, piercetaylorhibbs.com, or join my email list on Substack to download some free resources!

-PTH

ALSO BY THE AUTHOR

In Divine Company
Theological English
The Speaking Trinity & His Worded World
Finding God in the Ordinary
Struck Down but Not Destroyed
Sill, Silent, and Strong
Finding Hope in Hard Things
The Book of Giving
I Am a Human
The Great Lie
God of Words
Christmas Glory

ALSO BY THE AUTHOR

Borrowed Images: Prose Poems
word by Word: Poems Inspired by Scripture

1. See Pierce Taylor Hibbs, The Speaking Trinity & His Worded World: Why Language Is at the Center of Everything (Eugene, OR: Wipf & Stock, 2018); The Trinity, Language, and Human Behavior: A Reformed Exposition of the Language Theory of Kenneth L. Pike, Reformed Academic Dissertations (Phillipsburg, NJ: P&R, 2018).

2. C. S. Lewis, The Last Battle, book 7 of Chronicles of Narnia (New York: HarperCollins, 2004), 761.

3. Geerhardus Vos, Anthropology, vol. 2 of Reformed Dogmatics, ed. and trans. Richard B. Gaffin Jr. (Bellingham, WA: Lexham, 2014), 13.

4. C. S. Lewis, The Last Battle, from the final paragraph.

5. I first came across this term in the work of Vern Poythress. For more discussion, see Redeeming Sociology: A God-Centered Approach (Wheaton, IL: Crossway, 2011), 112–114.

6. Calvin discusses idols in his Institutes 1.11.

7. My attempt to do this is represented in Finding God in the Ordinary (Eugene, OR: Wipf & Stock, 2018).

8. "To claim to know something while thinking it to be independent of God (or to deny that there is a God) is to fail to know it for what it really is. Whatever it is, it is created and sustained by God at every moment." K. Scott Oliphint, Covenantal Apologetics: Principles and Practice in Defense of Our Faith (Wheaton, IL: Crossway, 2013), 44.

9. Rankin Wilbourne, Union with Christ: The Way to Know and Enjoy God (East Sussex, England: David C Cook, 2016), 34, Kindle edition.

10. Wilbourne, Union with Christ, 44.

11. Dumitru Stăniloae, The Holy Trinity: In the Beginning There Was Love, trans. Roland Clark (Bookline, MA: Holy Cross Orthodox, 2012), 16. Though I'm in a different theological tradition from him and disagree with elements of his doctrine of the Trinity (most notably the notions of monarchianism and the Eastern rejection of the biblical teaching that the Spirit proceeds from the Father and the Son), I have found his writing on the love of God helpful.

12. I get into this in The Speaking Trinity & His Worded World: Why Language Is at the Center of Everything (Eugene, OR: Wipf & Stock, 2018).

13. Timothy R. Jennings, The God-Shaped Brain: How Changing Your View of God Transforms Your Life, 2nd ed. (Downers Grove, IL: IVP, 2017), 47.

14. On giving as a perspective on who God is, who we are, and what the world is like, see The Book of Giving: How the God Who Gives Can Make Us Givers (Independently published, 2021).

15. "Heart Beat," Cleveland Clinic, accessed November 4, 2019, https://my.clevelandclinic.org/health/articles/17064-heart-beat.

16. On how we find shaping and hope in our hard things, see Pierce Taylor Hibbs, Finding Hope in Hard Things: A Positive Take on Suffering (Independently published, 2020).

17. Paul David Tripp, Suffering: Gospel Hope When Life Doesn't Make Sense (Wheaton, IL: Crossway, 2018), 208.

18. William B. Barcley, The Secret of Contentment (Phillipsburg, NJ: P&R, 2010), 30.

19. There are variations, of course. Francis Turretin, for instance, suggests that the three prongs of our being made in God's image are (1) the spirituality and immortality of the soul; (2) our original righteousness; and (3) our dominion over creation. Francis Turretin, Institutes of Elenctic Theology, ed. James T. Dennison, Jr., trans. George Musgrave Giger (Phillipsburg, NJ: P&R, 1992), 1:466. For the classic Reformed position, see Louis Berkhof, Systematic Theology, new ed. (Grand Rapids, MI: William B. Eerdmans, 1996), 203–07.

20. Geerhardus Vos, Anthropology, vol. 2 of Reformed Dogmatics, ed. and trans. Richard B. Gaffin Jr. (Bellingham, WA: Lexham, 2014), 13. I develop my view of this further in The Speaking Trinity & His Worded World: Why Language Is at the Center of Everything (Eugene, OR: Wipf & Stock, 2018).

21. "He is the Sun of being and all creatures are His fleeting rays." Herman Bavinck, The Wonderful Works of God: Instruction in the Christian Religion according to the Reformed Confession, trans. Henry Zylstra (Glenside, PA: Westminster Seminary Press, 2019), 116.

22. David Whyte, Consolations: The Solace, Nourishment, and Underlying Meaning of Everyday Words (Langley, WA: Many Rivers, 2018), 33.

23. The analogy I'm using here, when examined closely, would resemble tritheism, since God is not three different elements. He is three persons who share one essence. The analogy of water, ice, and vapor resembles modalism. There are no analogies for the Trinity that hold because we can't take something from creation and make it perfectly represent the Creator. The point of our limited analogies is to help us understand some facet of God's nature, all the while recognizing that words and images must bow before the God of glory.

24. Vern S. Poythress, The Mystery of the Trinity: A Trinitarian Approach to the Attributes of God (Phillipsburg, NJ: P&R, 2020), 163.

25. Herman Bavinck, The Wonderful Works of God: Instruction in the Christian Religion according to the Reformed Confession, trans. Henry Zylstra (Glenside, PA: Westminster Seminary Press, 2019), 127–128.

26. Poythress, The Mystery of the Trinity, 92.

27. Poythress, The Mystery of the Trinity, 94.

28. Poythress, The Mystery of the Trinity, 97.

29. Timothy R. Jennings, The God-Shaped Brain: How Changing Your View of God Transforms Your Life, 2nd ed. (Downers Grove, IL: IVP, 2017), 130.

30. See Poythress, The Mystery of the Trinity, 96–99.

31. Robert Letham, Systematic Theology (Wheaton, IL: Crossway, 2019), 609–611.

32. Marilyn McEntyre, Word by Word: A Daily Spiritual Practice (Grand Rapids, MI: Eerdmans, 2016), 7.

33. Herman Bavinck, The Wonderful Works of God: Instruction in the Christian Religion according to the Reformed Confession, trans. Henry Zylstra (Glenside, PA: Westminster Seminary Press, 2019), 8.

34. "Our surroundings are shot through with personality because all things are related to the infinitely personal God." Cornelius Van Til, In Defense of the Faith, vol. 2, A Survey of Christian Epistemology (Phillipsburg, NJ: Presbyterian and Reformed Publishing, 1969), 78.

35. Bavinck, The Wonderful Works of God, 127–28.

36. I will not go into the biblical evidence for oneness and threeness, since that has already been done well by others. I recommend Robert Letham's The Holy Trinity: In Scripture, History, Theology, and Worship, rev. and exp. ed. (Phillipsburg, NJ: P&R, 2019), 3–86; and John Frame's Systematic Theology: An Introduction to Christian Belief (Phillipsburg, NJ: P&R, 2013), 421–515.

37. Vern Sheridan Poythress, Redeeming Sociology: A God-Centered Approach (Wheaton, IL: Crossway, 2011), 15.

38. Pierce Taylor Hibbs, The Speaking Trinity & His Worded World: Why Language Is at the Center of Everything (Eugene, OR: Wipf & Stock, 2018).

39. Poythress, Redeeming Sociology, 24.

40. Douglas Kelly, Systematic Theology: Grounded in Holy Scripture and Understood in Light of the Church, vol. 1, The God Who Is: The Holy Trinity (Ross-shire, Scotland: Mentor, 2008), 487.

41. See Pierce Taylor Hibbs, "Words for Communion," Modern Reformation 25, no. 4 (July 1, 2016): 5–8.

42. For a history on the teaching of perichoresis, the mutual interpenetration of persons in the Godhead, see Letham, The Holy Trinity, 192–93; 279–80; 422–25; 439–40. See also Pierce Taylor Hibbs, "Closing the Gaps: Perichoresis and the Nature of Language," Westminster Theological Journal 78 (2016): 299–322.

43. Michael Reeves, Delighting in the Trinity: An Introduction to the Christian Faith (Downers Grove, IL: IVP Academic, 2012), 38. Ralph Smith notes, "To conceive of a god who does not know love, a god who has never shared, a god for whom a relationship with another is eternally irrelevant, is to conceive of an abstraction, an idea or a thing more than a person." Ralph A. Smith, Trinity & Reality: An Introduction to the Christian Faith (Moscow, ID: Canon, 2004), 18.

44. I speak generally here, since upon closer inspection, we would find much differentiation in ocean water.

45. On the unity and and diversity in the Trinity, see Cornelius Van Til, An Introduction to Systematic Theology: Prolegomena and the Doctrines of Revelation, Scripture, and God, 2nd ed., ed. William Edgar (Phillipsburg, NJ: P&R, 2007), 348, 353; The Defense of the Faith, 4th ed., ed. K. Scott Oliphint (Phillipsburg, NJ: P&R, 2008), 45–53; Vern S. Poythress, Redeeming Philosophy: A God-Centered Approach to the Big Questions (Wheaton, IL: Crossway, 2014), 57–58.

46. Abraham Kuyper, The Work of the Holy Spirit, trans. Henri De Vries (Chattanooga, TN: AMG, 1995), 542.

47. Adam McHugh, The Listening Life: Embracing Attentiveness in a World of Distraction (Downers Grove, IL: IVP, 2015).

48. On creation as a choral poem of God, see Vern S. Poythress, "Science as Allegory," The Works of John Frame and Vern Poythress, https://frame-poythress.org/science-as-allegory/.

49. Andreas J. Köstenberger, John, Baker Exegetical Commentary on the New Testament (Grand Rapids, MI: Baker Academic, 2004), 492.

50. BDAG, 230.

51. Andreas J. Köstenberger, *A Theology of John's Gospel and Letters*, Biblical Theology of the New Testament (Grand Rapids, MI: Zondervan, 2009), 248–49.

52. Richard Bauckham, *Gospel of Glory: Major Themes in Johannine Theology* (Grand Rapids, MI: Baker Academic, 2015), 36.

53. Herman N. Ridderbos, *The Gospel according to John: A Theological Commentary*, trans. John Vriend (Grand Rapids, MI: William B. Eerdmans, 1997), 560.

54. D. A. Carson, *The Gospel according to John*, Pillar New Testament Commentary (Grand Rapids, MI: Eerdmans, 1991), 568.

55. Carson, *The Gospel according to John*, 568.

56. On the importance of naming, see Vern S. Poythress, *In the Beginning Was the Word: Language—a God-Centered Approach* (Wheaton, IL: Crossway, 2009), 30–33; and Pierce Taylor Hibbs, *The Speaking Trinity & His Worded World: Why Language Is at the Center of Everything* (Eugene, OR: Wipf & Stock, 2018), 87–101.

57. Herman N. Ridderbos, *The Gospel according to John*, 561.

58. Köstenberger, *John*, 497.

59. John Owen, Communion with the Triune God, ed. Kelly M. Kapic and Justin Taylor (Wheaton, IL: Crossway, 2007), 94.

60. John Mark Comer, Live No Lies: Recognize and Resist the Three Enemies That Sabotage Your Peace (Colorado Springs, CO: Waterbrook, 2021), 151.

61. Vern S. Poythress, Interpreting Eden: A Guide to Faithfully Reading and Understanding Genesis 1–3 (Wheaton, IL: Crossway, 2019), 200.

62. Poythress, Interpreting Eden, 200.

63. J. Gresham Machen, Things Unseen: A Systematic Introduction to the Christian Faith and Reformed Theology (Glenside, PA: Westminster Seminary Press, 2020), 9.

64. Machen, Things Unseen, 13.

65. Rainer Maria Rilke, The Book of Hours, trans. Anita Barrows and Joanna Macy (New York: Riverhead, 2005), 53.

66. G. K. Beale, A New Testament Biblical Theology: The Unfolding of the Old Testament in the New (Grand Rapids, MI: Baker Academic, 2011), 465.

67. Dane Ortlund, Gentle and Lowly: The Heart of Christ for Sinners and Sufferers (Wheaton, IL: Crossway, 2020), 30.

68. John Mark Comer, The Ruthless Elimination of Hurry: How to Stay Emotionally Healthy and Spiritually Alive in the Chaos of the Modern World (Colorado Springs, CO: Waterbook, 2019), 70.

69. Mary Oliver, Upstream: Selected Essays (New York: Penguin, 2010), "Section One: Upstream."

70. Comer, The Ruthless Elimination of Hurry, 50.

71. Comer, The Ruthless Elimination of Hurry, 47.

72. Comer, The Ruthless Elimination of Hurry, 48–51.

73. "Americans Check Their Phones 96 Times a Day," Asurion, November 21, 2019, https://www.asurion.com/about/press-releases/americans-check-their-phones-96-times-a-day/.

74. Trevor Wheelwright, "Cell Phone Behavior in 2021: How Obsessed Are We?" Reviews.org, April 21, 2021, https://www.reviews.org/mobile/cell-phone-addiction/#:~:text=re%20not%20alone.-,On%20average%2C%20Americans%20check%20their%20phones%20262%20times%20per%20day,ve%20fallen%20into%20our%20screens.

75. I've written a review here: http://piercetaylorhibbs.com/gentle-and-lowly-by-dane-ortlund/.

76. Dane Ortlund, Gentle and Lowly: The Heart of Christ for Sinners and Sufferers (Wheaton, IL: Crossway, 2020), 18.

77. Ortlund, Gentle and Lowly, 19.

78. Ortlund, Gentle and Lowly, 20.

79. Ortlund, Gentle and Lowly, 21.

80. John Murray, Redemption Accomplished and Applied (Grand Rapids, MI: Eerdmans, 1955), 206.

81. A. W. Pink, Spiritual Union and Communion (Faithful Classic), Introduction, Kindle edition.

82. Rankin Wilbourne, Union with Christ: The Way to Know and Enjoy God (East Sussex, England: David C Cook, 2016), 11, Kindle edition.

83. Wilbourne, Union with Christ, 12, 13.

84. Wilbourne, Union with Christ, 15.

85. Wilbourne, Union with Christ, 74.

86. Wilbourne, Union with Christ, 75.

87. Wilbourne, Union with Christ, 81.

88. Iain Duguid, "Old Testament Hermeneutics," in Seeing Christ in All of Scripture: Hermeneutics at Westminster Theological Seminary, ed. Peter A. Lillback (Glenside, PA: Westminster Seminary Press, 2016), 17, 19.

89. Vern S. Poythress, Reading the Word of God in the Presence of God: A Handbook for Biblical Interpretation (Wheaton, IL: Crossway, 2016), 33.

90. Poythress, Reading the Word of God in the Presence of God, 235.

91. Poythress, Reading the Word of God in the Presence of God, 241–242.

92. This is why Poythress notes that these time reference tools are perspectivally related and coinhere with each other, p. 235.

93. I first saw this illustration in a Sunday school curriculum by Tim Keller.

94. He develops this idea in the context of his language theory in chapter 13 of Linguistic Concepts: An Introduction to Tagmemics (Lincoln, NE: University of Nebraska Press, 1982).

95. Dane Ortlund, Gentle and Lowly: The Heart of Christ for Sinners and Sufferers (Wheaton, IL: Crossway, 2020), 18.

96. Edmund P. Clowney, Christian Meditation: What the Bible Teaches about Meditation and Spiritual Exercises (Vancouver: Regent College Publishing, 1979), 46.

97. Clowney, Christian Meditation, 46.

98. Clowney, Christian Meditation, 47.

99. Clowney, Christian Meditation, 91.

100. Adam S. McHugh, The Listening Life: Embracing Attentiveness in a World of Distraction (Downers Grove, IL: IVP, 2015), 67.

101. McHugh, The Listening Life, 81.

102. Sinclair Ferguson, "Our New Affection," Ligonier Ministries, accessed July 31, 2021, https://www.ligonier.org/learn/articles/our-new-affection/.

103. This is one of the central messages I harp on in Struck Down but Not Destroyed and Finding Hope in Hard Things.

104. Andrew Peterson, The Monster in the Hollows, book 3 of The Wingfeather Saga (Colorado Springs, CO: Waterbrook, 2011), 54.

105. Ferguson, "Our New Affection."

106. Rankin Wilbourne, Union with Christ: The Way to Know and Enjoy God (East Sussex, England: David C Cook, 2016), 46, Kindle edition.

107. See my article, "You Are They: Human Identity and the Trinity," Westminster Magazine 2, no. 1 (Fall 2021): 60–64.

108. Christian Wiman, My Bright Abyss: Meditation of a Modern Believer (New York: Farrar, Straus and Giroux, 2013), 23–24.

109. Eugene H. Peterson, *A Long Obedience in the Same Direction: Discipleship in an Instant Society*, 2nd ed. (Downers Grove, IL: IVP, 2000), 162.

110. Sinclair Ferguson, *Lessons from the Upper Room: The Heart of the Savior* (Sanford, FL: Ligonier Ministries, 2021), 213.

111. Francis Chan, *Until Unity* (Colorado Springs, CO: David C Cook, 2021), 15–16.

112. Christian Wiman, *My Bright Abyss: Meditation of a Modern Believer* (New York: Ferrar, Straus and Giroux, 2013), 29.

113. Chan, *Until Unity*, 26.

www.ingramcontent.com/pod-product-compliance
Lightning Source LLC
Chambersburg PA
CBHW050332010526
44119CB00004B/129